LESSONS LEARNED

Steve Mawhorter

LESSONS LEARNED

After 20 years of being a Biblical Counselor

STEVE MAWHORTER

Lessons Learned by Steve Mawhorter
Copyright © 2020 by Steve Mawhorter
All Rights Reserved.
ISBN: 978-1-59755-585.2

Published by: ADVANTAGE BOOKS™
Longwood, Florida, USA
www.advbookstore.com

This book and parts thereof may not be reproduced in any form, stored in a retrieval system or transmitted in any form by any means (electronic, mechanical, photocopy, recording or otherwise) without prior written permission of the author, except as provided by United States of America copyright law.

Scripture taken from the NEW AMERICAN STANDARD BIBLE®, Copyright © 1960, 1962, 1963, 1968, 1971, 1972, 1973, 1975, 1977, 1995 by The Lockman Foundation. Used by permission.

Library of Congress Catalog Number: 2020939753

First Printing: July 2020
20 21 22 23 24 25   10 9 8 7 6 5 4 3 2 1
Printed in the United States of America

Table of Contents

SECTION 1: WHAT I'VE LEARNED IN COUNSELING THAT CAN HELP YOUR MINISTRY

CHAPTER 1: LIAR, LIAR, PANTS ON FIRE **13**
- MEET CATHY AND CARL 13
- THE PRINCIPLE 15
- HOW THIS CAN HELP YOUR MINISTRY 15

CHAPTER 2: YOUR SIN WILL FIND YOU OUT **17**
- MEET THE BOB AND BETTY 17
- THE PRINCIPLE 18
- HOW THIS CAN HELP YOUR MINISTRY 19

CHAPTER 3: PEOPLE DO DIE FOR LACK OF INSTRUCTION **21**
- MEET DAVID 21
- THE PRINCIPLE 22
- HOW THIS CAN HELP YOUR MINISTRY 22

CHAPTER 4: SHOULD I TELL HER? **25**
- MEET FRED 26
- THE PRINCIPLES 27
- HOW THIS CAN HELP YOUR MINISTRY 28

CHAPTER 5: GOD TOLD ME AND MY CHURCH CONFIRMED IT **29**
- MEET ROSA 29
- THE PRINCIPLE 31
- HOW THIS CAN HELP YOUR MINISTRY 31

CHAPTER 6: SERIOUSLY? YOU DIDN'T THINK I NEEDED TO KNOW THAT? **33**
- MEET BRIAN AND PAM 33
- THE PRINCIPLES 36
- HOW THIS CAN HELP YOUR MINISTRY 37

CHAPTER 7: TIMING IS EVERYTHING **39**
- THE PRINCIPLES 40
- HOW THIS WILL HELP YOUR MINISTRY 41

CHAPTER 8: ARE YOU THE RIGHT PERSON? **43**
- MEET CLARA AND ELLEN 44
- THE PRINCIPLE 46
- HOW THIS CAN HELP YOUR MINISTRY 47

CHAPTER 9: SWALLOW HARD AND TELL THE TRUTH 49
Meet some counselees 49
The principle 51
How this can help your ministry 52

CHAPTER 10: WHAT? ME SIN? NEVER 53
Meet Alex and Barbara 53
The principle 54
How this can help your ministry 56

CHAPTER 11: I SWEAR TO GOD, I DIDN'T DO IT! 57
Meet Tina and Aaron 57
The principles 59
How this can help your ministry 60

CHAPTER 12: TEAR UP THOSE PAPERS 61
Meet Chad and Maria and Ron and Kimberly 61
The principle 63
How this can help your ministry 63

CHAPTER 13: PUT THOSE LABELS WHERE THEY BELONG 65
Meet Eric 65
The principles 68
How this can help your ministry 68

CHAPTER 14: START WITH HIM 69
Meet Bob and Betty 69
The principles 69
How this can help your ministry 71

CHAPTER 15: I ONLY DO IT ONCE IN A WHILE 73
Meet addicts 74
The principles 75
How this can help your ministry 76

CHAPTER 16: WHAT'S THE RUSH? 79
Meet Ed and Roberta 79
The principle 80
How this can help your ministry 81

SECTION 2: MESSAGES OF HOPE

CHAPTER 17: CAN YOUR MARRIAGE SURVIVE AN AFFAIR? 85
- MEET HEATHER AND DOUG 85
- THE PRINCIPLES 87
- HOW THIS CAN HELP YOUR MINISTRY 88

CHAPTER 18: YOU NEVER KNOW 91
- MEET BEN AND EMMA 91
- THE PRINCIPLE 93
- HOW THIS CAN HELP YOUR MINISTRY 93

CHAPTER 19: WOMEN ARE NOT COMPLICATED 95
- MEET HOWARD AND HEATHER 95
- THE PRINCIPLE 97
- HOW THIS CAN HELP YOUR MINISTRY 98

CHAPTER 20: I DON'T THINK I CAN TAKE ANYMORE! 99
- MEET HARRY AND WANDA 99
- THE PRINCIPLE 103
- HOW THIS CAN HELP YOUR MINISTRY 103

CHAPTER 21: SAULS INTO PAULS 105
- MEET ELAINE 105
- THE PRINCIPLE 107
- HOW THIS CAN HELP YOUR MINISTRY 107

CHAPTER 22: GUESS WHO DOES OUR GRIEF COUNSELING? 109
- MEET ROBERT 109
- THE PRINCIPLE 111
- HOW THIS CAN HELP YOUR MINISTRY 111

CHAPTER 23: DO PEOPLE REALLY GET SAVED IN COUNSELING EVERY YEAR? 113
- MEET PETER AND MARY 113
- THE PRINCIPLE 115
- HOW THIS CAN HELP YOUR MINISTRY 116

CHAPTER 24: THE POWER OF PRAYER 119
- MEET GARRY 119
- MEET CHRISSY 120
- THE PRINCIPLES 122
- HOW THIS CAN HELP YOUR MINISTRY 123

CHAPTER 25: TAKE THE CALL! MAKE THE CALL! 125
Meet Terry 125
How this can help your ministry 126

SECTION 3: PRACTICAL WISDOM FOR YOUR MINISTRY

CHAPTER 26: FOLLOW THE CLOUD 131
Our story at NorthCreek Church 131

CHAPTER 27: HOW TO START A BIBLICAL COUNSELING MINISTRY IN YOUR CHURCH . 137
The principles 137

CHAPTER 28: HOW DO I FIND PEOPLE WHO CAN HELP ME HELP MY PEOPLE? 141
What you're looking for on a spiritual level 141
What you're looking for on a practical level 142
How do you go about finding them? 143
Four final considerations 144

CHAPTER 29: THERE'S A LIMIT 147
How this can help your ministry 149

CHAPTER 30: SOMETIMES, IT'S GOING TO GET PERSONAL 151
Meet Paul, the lover 152
How this can help your ministry 154

CHAPTER 31: DON'T DO IT! 157
Meet Brian 157
Five reasons you shouldn't, just for her benefit 158
Three reasons you shouldn't, for your benefit 160
How this can help your ministry 161

CHAPTER 32: WHEN DO YOU CUT 'EM LOOSE? 163
Meet Jerry and Melinda 163
Questions to ask yourself 164

CHAPTER 33: MUCH ADO ABOUT NOTHING 169
Meet Casey and Kristen 169
The principle 172
How this can help your ministry 172

CHAPTER 34: CHURCH DISCIPLINE, DOES THAT REALLY WORK? 173
Meet Fred and Ethel 174
How this can help your ministry 176

CHAPTER 35: SHOULD I WORK WITH A DOCTOR OR A PSYCHIATRIST? 177

MEET TOM AND KIM 177
THE PRINCIPLES 178
HOW THIS CAN HELP YOUR MINISTRY 179

Steve Mawhorter

Section 1

What I've learned in counseling that can help your ministry

Steve Mawhorter

Lessons Learned

Chapter 1

Liar, liar, pants on fire

(1 Pet. 1:22; Gal. 6:9-10)

Meet Cathy and Carl

Cathy and Carl are believers and attend a bible teaching church. They are young and in good health, with young children all who attend a solid Christian school. Carl works to provide. Cathy's a stay-at-home Mom. From the outside, everything looks great, right? Well, looks can be deceiving and in this case, they were. By the time they got to me, they had become very distant from each other and he was having an affair.

Surprisingly, Cathy was very willing to put the marriage back together, but Carl was stuck in his affair. He would say, "I love my wife, but I am *in love* with my mistress, too." I've heard that a hundred times. In my head, I want to scream out, *you're not in love with your mistress. You're in love with yourself and how she makes you feel about yourself! It's just lust, buddy!* Ugh, I digress. He was right about one thing. He was stuck, stuck in his selfish, sinful pattern, demanding from God that he be with someone he was "in love with."

I had met with each of them individually one time and heard their stories, which were largely the same. The problem was that though she was willing to give it a try, he was not willing to leave his mistress. Now what, right? Well, I took an unconventional approach. Even though they were not part of our church, I decided to give it a whirl. I thought to myself, let's see if God is up to something here. So, I began counseling them together.

During the next few months, he began to show signs of softening. We had been going through *Strengthening Your Marriage, God's Way* by Wayne Mack, which forces you in the Word. They were soaking it up. They spent hours together going over the homework and then hours with me discussing it. There was hope, but he was not ready to break off the affair, so we were not quite out of the woods yet.

Though Carl appeared hopeful, Cathy was understandably hesitant, fearing that he was hiding his true feelings about his mistress from her. And she had good reasons to be. There was very little intimacy. He was very needy and overly sensitive. One mistake by her and it would upset him. He was largely absent from the home, traveling for his job or on one of his fun adventures. He was quite the pleasure seeker. Duh, right?! On top of that, he was still stubborn, proud, and arrogant. You can imagine how hard this was for her. Yet, there was still some hope because we were still meeting, and they were still doing their homework.

Finally, after one of our sessions, after 3 months of counseling, he finally agreed he would end it with his mistress, but he wasn't ready to move back home yet. So he broke it off with his mistress and moved in with a friend.

We continued to work through the book, but I didn't see much softening on his end and, understandably so, I saw little trust on hers either. He remained needy, and harsh in his behavior towards her. He was often not at home. She was trying be patient with God's timing. I continued to pray that God would soften Carl's heart towards Cathy and increase his passion for her. I prayed that God would help Cathy remain patient and that she would learn to trust God with her fears of him never coming home.

After 6 months of meetings, he finally came home. He apologized to her and to their children. All was good. We finished the book. He was pursuing his wife and she was responding. I followed up a month later and they seemed to be doing very well. Intimacy was difficult as can be expected but they were worshiping, fellowshipping, and praying together. The end, right? Wrong.

A month later, I met with her and he had not only gone back to his mistress, but he confessed that he had never left her and had been with her the entire time of their separation and our counseling. It was all a sham. He was a total liar.

Because I did not see any evidence of faith in Carl, I recommended that Cathy let him go as you would an unbeliever and I declined his strange request for friendship from me. Now, that was the end. Sad, but true.

The principle

Why is this story in this book? How is this helpful? Because you need to know that people that look like good people, and even people that ARE good people, will look you right in the eye and lie right to your face like you are some chump on the street asking for spare change while they have a cigarette in one hand and a beer in the other. Okay, given that this is true, what do we do with that information?

Do we look at everyone we counsel with suspicion? Do we assume they are telling partial truths or total lies, or do we trust them with their words and let the cookie crumble however it crumbles?

I'm not sure you'll like my answer, but I believe it's possible to take people at their word even though they may not be telling you everything they should be telling you. Bad people lie but even good people lie sometimes, and for lots of reasons. We have to let God have control of that. We are not called to discern their lies. We are called to love, and love believes. So believe, but also believe they are not necessarily telling you everything. Let God have the rest of it. It will come out when He is good and ready.

How this can help your ministry

I did what God had called me to do. I loved Carl and Cathy. I was devoted to them. I taught, loved, encouraged, exhorted, comforted, challenged, and prayed for them. I was faithful to the end. Did Carl burn me? Yes. He would not be the last. Others did and more will, but I will remain faithful no matter how much pain they inflict.

When your people lie to your face, some of it will hurt only a little because there is not much of a relationship there. Others will hurt more than you can imagine because there is a deep relationship there. So what?! Our call is to love! So, do it even though you may end on the bitter end of relationship like this one. Do not be deterred from your highest calling, that is, to love your people (1 Peter 1:22).

Galatians 6:9-10, "Let us not become weary in doing good, for at the proper time we will reap a harvest if we do not give up. [10]Therefore, as we have opportunity, let us do good to all people, especially to those who belong to the family of believers." Press on brothers and sisters.

Steve Mawhorter

Lessons Learned

Chapter 2

Your sin will find you out

(Numbers 32: 22-23)

Meet the Bob and Betty.

To say the least, Betty lived a checkered past. Raised in an unhealthy home, split family, financial troubles, and a mother that encouraged sexual experimentation. Her troubles began as a young girl and continued into her 30s before she finally found the Lord and a man she could trust, Bob. He was a wealthy, good looking, hard-working, honest, faithful, pure guy, who had waited all his life for a woman that loved God and him. When they met, there was an instant connection and a little over a year later, they married.

Soon after, however, they began to have troubles communicating over, guess what . . . finances. They began to get collection notices in the mail. She began to find credit cards she didn't know about. Income that he used to get from investments were no longer coming in and they were unable to make the payments on their bills so the credit began to grow and they had begun borrowing money from friends. She was scared and incensed to say the least, and for good reason.

I brought them in and looked over their finances. He showed me his balance sheet, which showed that although they are cash poor, they were asset rich. This is common in the great state of California. At any time during my adult life, you could sell your home in California, take the equity, and buy a home in most any other state for cash. They were fine, so I thought.

I began to question him a little more on this because he said he would check on all these investments, all with names I'd never heard of before. Though I was a bit nervous, I'd known him for a long time and trusted him and I implored her to trust him as well. She did, for the most part.

Additionally, he began having trouble at his job and was let go. After months of trying he finally got a job, though it didn't pay well.

Sad to say, that after over a year of counseling, he finally began to open up a little, telling us that he's a bad person, wondering if he was saved. This sounded like humility talking, but was it? She continued to get counseling for herself as he became more and more hard to communicate with. She nor we could get him to do much of anything when it came to counseling homework.

Two years into counseling, the debt continued to pile up and the creditors continued to call. Bob and Betty were selling assets at bargain rates, though there wasn't much to sell anyway. And, more lies were coming to the surface. A resume described him in glowing ways that were totally untrue and ripped off from a website or made up out of thin air. He, who was one of the most mild-mannered guys you'll ever meet, starting throwing fits of rage, even throwing chairs.

Finally, it all began to come out. He had been lying about everything to everyone for years. He didn't own the home they were living in. He had not paid his HOA fees or property taxes for years. He had not made a payment on the home for over 3 1/2 years. He had not filed tax returns for years. And, he had not held a job for years. The job he supposedly lost, he never had. The whole thing was a sham. There were no investments. He was flat broke when they got married. She had married a complete liar. He had been fooling her and all his friends.

The principle

Though this story is on the "crazy" side, it is a common one. You find it mostly when affairs come to the surface. People will write letters to their lovers, and then leave them on the printer. They will view pornography and forget to close out the program or sign off their computer. They'll text their spouse, thinking they're texting their lover. It's amazing how many ways, sooner or later, sin will be brought to the surface.

Numbers 32: 22-23 says this, "this land shall be yours for a possession before the Lord. But if you will not do so, behold, you have sinned against the Lord, and be sure your sin will find you out." This was 40 years after Israel had been in the same position ready to take the land God had promised them, but they were once again hesitant. Moses tells them that if they don't trust Him and take the land, their sin will find them out, meaning sin will come after them as it did Cain when he fought with God over his offering.

Sin will one day find us all out. It is the sins we commit that will one day haunt us. Sin always leads to more sin, pain, misery, regret upon regret, guilt, shame, and so on. And, sooner or later, our gracious, loving, merciful, all-loving God, will bring it to the light. This is when true healing can actually begin.

How this can help your ministry

How does this help us as counselors, friends, and mentors? If you suspect you are not being told the truth and there is more going on than is being said, you may very well be right. Sin loves to hide but God will expose it in His good timing. In the story, there was much this woman needed to learn that she would not have learned had the truth come out in the first weeks of marriage. If she found out right away, I have little doubt that she would have bolted right away. The two years of counseling was incredibly painful for her but in the end, it has matured her. It made her more ready to be gracious and merciful.

Today, they remain married. Who'd have thought that? They are still working through their communication issues, and paying down that debt, but they are together. Only God! Be patient with your counselees and with God's timing. He'll bring it out when he's good and ready.

1 Thess. 5:14, "We urge you, brethren, admonish the unruly, encourage the fainthearted, help the weak, be patient with everyone."

Steve Mawhorter

Chapter 3

People do die for lack of instruction

(Prov. 5:23)

Meet David

My wife and I live in a home that faces 2 streets that both end in cul de sacs with a driveway that comes out on both streets, and we live behind a large high school. The students have found it a quicker getaway to drive up our street and through our driveway to come out the other side. Great for them. Not so great for us. Frequently during the year, students will actually do this. They ignore the fact that they are driving on our property to save only a couple of minutes. The problem is, our driveway has a retaining wall with wood posts on it and it's a bit of a tight drive to avoid those posts. Though they usually make it fine, occasionally, it doesn't work out that way.

One day, my wife and I just happened to be standing in our driveway where the students can't see us and one of them (David) came driving through our driveway. When he came to the place that has a tight turn, he looked over and saw us standing there. Instead of hitting the break and backing out, he panicked and slammed on the gas, ramming his big sedan into the wood post on the retaining wall. Well, that was the end of that post.

I walked over to the young man and calmed him down. "It's ok son. Just give me your phone number and I'll call your Dad and we can work something out. It'll only cost a couple hundred dollars to fix." He gave me his number and off he went, nervous as all get out.

Later that day, I called his father and asked him what he'd like to do to take care of it. I was even willing to help if he wanted it. I felt bad for the kid. The father responded with this, "nothing." I said, "what do you mean nothing? You're not going to fix it or involve him in helping to fix it? Nothing?" He said, "nope." I was so stunned that I really had almost no response, which is rare for a pastor, right? We don't ordinarily have nothing to say. With that, we hung up, and never spoke again.

Late one evening, two years later, I heard a story that brought chills to my spine and sadness to my heart. Two young boys decided to do a little drag racing on a street where there are rarely other cars that late in the night. It seemed safe to them. They sat in their respective cars, stared each other down and hit the gas. They headed down about a mile and something happened. One of the cars lost control and swerved off to the side and into a house on the corner.

Thankfully, no one was harmed in the home, though the entire front of the house was trashed. Sadly, the boy in the car, was pronounced dead in the hospital only hours later. That boy was the boy whose father did not make him pay for his mistake on my driveway.

The principle

What did I learn from this? The Bible means business when it says they will die for lack of instruction (Prov. 5:23). Yes, they will, and he did. I have often wondered how that boy and his family's life would have been different if that father had taken advantage of the opportunity that God gave him and taught his son a lesson. It would have saved his life for sure.

God means what He says. There are a plethora of warnings throughout the pages of Scripture. In the book of Proverbs alone, we are warned about lust, backsliding, laziness, jealousy, greed, etc., etc. When He says He hates divorce, He does. When He says that if you go to sleep on your anger, you give Satan a foothold, you do. When He says you reap what you sow, you do. God means what he says so boldly and lovingly tell your people the truth.

How this can help your ministry

I am not the only one with a story like this. We've all heard of them. That said, why do we as counselors and pastors not pound harder on our pulpits and beg our parents to teach their children whenever and wherever we can? Why are we afraid to say something that will hurt our counselees feelings or push them away? Be bold. Speak the truth, in love (Eph. 4:15).

Lessons Learned

Tell your people and tell your people to tell their kids every time God gives them opportunities like this. You won't be sorry for over-teaching but you may be sorry for under-teaching. And, rarely have I ever had someone not come back to counseling because I told them the truth about what God says in the Bible. The fact is, they often already know it and just need someone in authority to verbalize it for them. The truth becomes comforting to them.

Deut. 6:4-8, "Hear, O Israel! The Lord is our God, the Lord is one! 5 You shall love the Lord your God with all your heart and with all your soul and with all your might. 6 These words, which I am commanding you today, shall be on your heart. 7 You shall teach them diligently to your sons and shall talk of them when you sit in your house and when you walk by the way and when you lie down and when you rise up. 8 You shall bind them as a sign on your hand and they shall be as frontals on your forehead.

Eph. 6:4b, "bring them up in the discipline and instruction of the Lord."

Steve Mawhorter

Chapter 4

Should I tell her?

(Prov. 28:13)

    Newsflash! Christians or not, married or single, people make major errors in their lives. Not often, but often enough. When it happens, what should they do? Should they confess or should they take it to their grave. It's a great question and sooner or later, someone is going to ask you this very question. In these two stories, you'll discover why it's sometimes best to have the pastor present when a spouse is going to confess their sin.

    I've already written a chapter noting how the sin you're engaging in will eventually find you out, meaning, sooner or later, it will come to the surface. Your wife will find a note, "miss you." You'll leave the phone on and she'll see a text, "looking forward to seeing you again." You'll turn your computer off but not close out a picture you were looking at online. You'll forget to scrub your history and she'll finally look at. She'll see phone numbers on your bill that she doesn't recognize. You'll go way over your cell data. Or, maybe even the other woman will call your wife. Out of nowhere, the police may even knock on your door. These are all actual ways the truth has come out in my counseling. Need I remind you of anymore? It's going to come out somehow, but there's another way it comes out.

    It comes out by confession. Good Christians fall, people. We are all one slip away. There is a chink in everyone's armor, a crack in everyone's dam. As the song says, we are all prone to wander and if it were not for God's protection, we would all fall. So, get off your high horse now and give people some grace.

    Proverbs 28:13 says, "He who conceals his transgressions will not prosper, but he who confesses and forsakes them will find compassion." The best-case scenario is not only that this sin comes out by confession, but it is also always best case that it is met with compassion rather than the pride and arrogance that I have seen so much of.

I don't have enough fingers and toes to account for the many men (and a few women) who have come to me with unconfessed sin, asking me if they should tell their wives, husbands, or parents. What would you tell them if they came to you?

Over the years, I would say that almost all of my fellow leaders in the biblical counseling world, would tell them that they *must* tell their spouse. They would say the injured spouse deserves to know. Or, they say, "there is no unity where there is secrecy." They would say that if you don't, it will always stunt your growth. You'll know in your soul every time you worship that you are keeping something from your wife that she deserves to know. You'll live in fear that she will find out some other way and there will be hell to pay. The list of reasons to tell could go on but I want the other side to be considered here, too. Let me do that by illustration.

Meet Fred

Fred was a super nice guy, very successful in his field, married with children. He's a Christian attending a solid church. He comes to me with his confession. Ten years ago, before he became a believer (though he thought he was at the time), he had a one-time sexual encounter with someone at his work. His marriage was not in great shape when it happened. He was stressed by his work, and it was late at night. She came on to him and he was ill-prepared to turn her away. By the way, one of my female counselors once told me something that I'd never heard before but believe to be largely true. She said, "men are no match for women. If they want it, they will get it from you." Yikes, that is scary. Lord, lead me not into temptation, right? I see why that prayer is there. Anyway, back to Fred.

Fred was no match for this woman. He was vulnerable and he fell. It was one time, ten years ago. Fast forward to the day of his confession and his marriage is still not the best but it's not the worst either. Fred is fairly new in his faith and he is growing by leaps and bounds. He's feeling guilty because he is keeping this event from his wife and the weight of that burden is really getting to him. He wants to know if he should confess and he asked me straight up. Should I tell her?

This, mind you, is before I even started the counseling ministry at our church. I was working on my Masters' degree, but I was in no way ready for a question like this. So, my answer was to do what he felt the Lord was leading him to. My answer today would be different, though you may not like it. Here's what happened to Fred after he confessed.

Fred's wife threw a fit. There was no compassion, no grace, no mercy and no love. Instead, there was hatred, pride, and arrogance. Fred's wife packed up their kids and left the state. He had to quit his job and find something closer to where they were. His confession wrecked his life. Thankfully, years later, Fred would remarry and have another set of children. He would restore his career and find joy in his walk and in his marriage.

You say, well it all turned out great. Well, if all you care about is where they are at now, yeah, he's doing well. But what about the years of pain he endured? What about his children from his first marriage? What about his ex-wife and the shame she must have felt for being a single mom from a failed marriage? Can you just imagine for a moment the pain everyone felt? It was excruciating. Fred's conscience was clean, but his life was tragic for years. So, should he have told her?

The principles

Well folks, there is no black and white answer to this question. Some of you are still stuck on "you must tell." Well, what if it was 50 years ago and she was on her death bed? Should he tell her then? Or, what if it was just one kiss and it was a long time ago? Should he tell her? What if her father had left her mother for another woman, should he tell her when it was ten years ago (or twenty or thirty) and it has nothing to do with their marriage today?

Listen, I am not advocating lying to your spouse or covering your tracks. That is very, very dangerous. If you have committed adultery and it's recent, you need to tell your spouse. If you've been watching pornography for a lengthy enough time that you need some help, you need to tell her. In fact, if you've viewed it once, you need to tell someone for sure, just maybe not her yet. Or, maybe she's the best one. You'll have to decide that. You say, well, how do we know whether to tell or who to tell or when to tell? Great question!

I think there are 3 principles that are helpful here. First, James 5:16 says, "Therefore, confess your sins to one another, and pray for one another so that you may be healed. The effective prayer of a righteous man can accomplish much." Yes, you should confess, but to whom, it doesn't say. Don't add, confess your sins *to your wife*. It does not say that. There's just more to it than a blanket statement, "you must confess to your wife." By the way, I guarantee that no man confesses every sin to his wife or he'd be telling her he has had a lustful thought every week, much less every day, or every hour. So, get off your high horse about confessing your sins to your wife.

Second, is the law of love. It's simple. What is the most loving thing to do? How will your confession benefit your wife? Maybe it will. Maybe it won't. Seek the Lord on this. Spend time in the Word and prayer for days, if not weeks and perhaps even fast. This leads me to my third principle, get some counsel.

Proverbs 15:22 says, "Without consultation, plans are frustrated, but with many counselors they succeed. Proverbs 11:14 says, "Where there is no guidance the people fall, but in abundance of counselors there is victory." These are proverbial in nature but make their point. Get some advice.

How this can help your ministry

Go to your pastor on this one. He has the experience in knowing how to handle it. He can even be there during the confession to minister to her and help her understand how this could happen. He can pray with and for both of you together. It can be a time of healing instead of torture. He can bring his wife or a trusted counselor with him to comfort her and to give her hope. Trust me on this people. This can be a very important step in your healing. Get advice from the shepherd who is responsible for caring for your soul. We love you. Let us love you.

Lessons Learned

Chapter 5

God told me and my church confirmed it

(1 Timothy 3:16-17, 2 Peter 1:3, Hebrews 1:1-2)

Meet Rosa

This chapter contains four stories that will demonstrate how I've learned that charismatics are very hard to counsel, the first one being the longest and most sordid.

Rosa came to me from a somewhat charismatic church in our area. They didn't roll in the aisles, bark like dogs, or do the "holy laughter" thing, but they were definitely charismatic. Though they love the Bible, they also believe that God talks to them. You may have heard someone say they've, "heard a word from the Lord." My first story illustrates this.

Rosa was struggling with anxiety and depression so she went to a local psychologist. She told the psychologist that she *kind of* remembered or thought that *maybe* her mother had abused her when she was a child. Putting two and two together, the psychologist determined that she probably had what is known as repressed memory syndrome (RMS).

RMS is where your memories have been unconsciously blocked due to the memory being associated with a high level of stress or trauma. Some call this dissociative amnesia, which basically means that due to high levels of stress in your life, you are unable to recall certain important events about your childhood.

For Rosa and the psychologist, this meant that the difficulties surrounding her marriage and family had caused her to block out things that may have happened when she was very young. With lots of therapy, the psychologist helped her remember that she was indeed abused by her mother who the psychologist claimed hit Rosa with a frying pan when she was six months old in the crib. You gasp, why would anyone believe the psychologist? Well, Rosa didn't.

However, Rosa was both confused and uncomfortable with the conclusions of the psychologist, so she went to her church. Surely, they would help her sort it out.

The women of this charismatic church gathered around her and prayed over her. After they concluded their prayer for her, they confirmed that the psychologist was correct and that God had told them (there's your "word from the Lord") that Rosa was indeed abused just as the psychologist had said. This devastated Rosa.

Rosa, at the request of the women at her church, then confronted her mother and father. They vehemently denied the claims. What is Rosa to do now?! Disgruntled with her psychologist and her church, she came to us. We told her the truth. RMS is a lie that began with Sigmund Freud and God does not talk to people the way the women in her church had said. We encouraged her to drop all of that and let's just see how we can help her with her anxiety and depression.

Sadly, we only met a few times because she was unable to let go of the thoughts that were placed into her head that she had received from her sophisticated psychologist and her church hearing a word from God. We could not really help her, so counseling ended.

Now, onto my second story.

Ralph (a good tongue-talking charismatic) and Terry (not charismatic) were another couple I counseled for many months. Ralph was sure his wife was having or had had an affair because God told him so. While she was no doubt good with men, she very strongly denied any wrongdoing. Ralph, though, believing that God speaks to him, would not let this go. His suspicion eventually drove Terry away and they ended up divorced.

Then I had Shannon. Shannon was a believer who loved God's Word, but she also loved God's personal words to her even more. By that, I mean that Shannon loved what she believed God was telling her, privately, over and above the actual words of God on the pages of our Bibles. She believed God wanted her to feed her children a certain type of food. Her husband disagreed, saying they didn't have the money for what she wanted for the kids. He begged her to buy food they could afford. She refused, saying she would be sinning by submitting to him. They also ended in divorce.

The last one is John. Super guy but again charismatic leanings. He was no doubt stuck in a bad marriage to an alcoholic wife who had no desire for church. John also loved God and the Bible. But, he came to a point where he firmly believed that God was telling him he should leave his wife and he did and it fractured the family.

The principle

This one is pretty clear, isn't it? People who believe that God talks to them in some fashion other than the principles on the pages of our bibles will eventually raise their own "words from God" above those found in the Bible. And, if you can't pull them out of those charismatic leanings, counseling won't go anywhere because in their minds, your words conflict with theirs from God and you will lose that battle every time.

How this can help your ministry

Teach the people of your church the importance of the doctrine of the inspiration, inerrancy, authority, and sufficiency of Scripture. Remind them that the canon is closed. And, help them understand that the voices in their head or the feelings they have about what God is telling them is not coming from God. It's coming from their own imaginations and the idolatrous desires that are ruling their hearts (Ja. 1:14-15).

Biblical counselors agree that everything we need to know for salvation *and* sanctification has been revealed completely and finally in Jesus Christ and, through the teaching of the apostles and prophets, has been recorded in Scripture (1 Timothy 3:16-17, 2 Peter 1:3, Hebrews 1:1-2).

Therefore, we don't need any further prophecy, or "word from the Lord," or "word of knowledge" to inform us as to what God's will is. The concept surrounding continuing revelation is nonsense and will only lead people away from the one true sufficient revelation, that we already have, the Bible. And, if you're going to counsel a charismatic, start your counseling with these biblical concepts. You won't get very far with them unless they change their minds about this.

Lessons Learned

Chapter 6

Seriously? You didn't think I needed to know that?

(Jam. 5:16; 1 Jn. 1:9; Prov. 28:13)

Meet Brian and Pam

This was a seemingly solid couple. Brian had a great job, and was in a good bible study. Pam served in ministry and was also in a bible study. Together, they raised their sweet kids. The only way you could detect that maybe there might be something off here is that neither were close to anyone, especially her, which can be very revealing. It's normal for men to be somewhat disconnected but it is not normal for a woman. Other than that, these two looked like every other normal couple at your church.

Then one day, in a moment of exasperation, Brian came to see me. He had found his wife flirting on Facebook with another man. I would later find out that she had been unfaithful once before. In fact, she had been unfaithful before and after they were married. This one, would be a third . . . that we know of.

He felt emasculated. He totally shut down. She had complete control over him.

For many reasons, it was an odd first meeting. Not only because it was so unexpected but because even though he had all the information regarding her most recent triste, she continued to deny it. Normally, when one is found out, there are tears of contrition, sometimes even wailing and sobbing. The person usually feels great shame. Not this time. In fact, she not only denied the online affair, but she blamed him for it, whatever *it* was.

I let them go that evening, not sure they'd be coming back, but they did. They had a great talk. They listened to each other. He forgave her. And, they committed to right the relationship. They had good, long talks together, but there were three things I heard that made me cautious.

One, she was angry that he told me what she did. When people are upset that their sin has come to the surface, that's not usually a good sign. Most people who are truly repentant will tell you anything. They want out of their sin and know that a full confession is the only road that leads there.

Two, rather than accept responsibility, and feel sorrow over her sin, she would say she felt beat down by it. This is common for the perp. They are always the first to be ready to move on. It's the victim who needs time and attention, a lot of time, and a lot of attention. Both people need compassion but it's the victim who really needs it. She was so engulfed in her own desire to put the problems behind them, that she cared little about how he felt. This, too, is very common. Perps just can't understand how hard it is for the victim and I mean that literally. Unless you've been one, how can you know how it feels, right?

Three, rather than taking responsibility for her sin, she blamed two sources. One, she blamed it on their unresolved differences and two, she blamed it on her upbringing, which involved both domestic violence and an early exposure to sexuality. Now, before you throw this book in the fire, let me explain why this bothered me.

First, by blaming it on resolved differences, she was actually blaming him for not resolving them. What she was actually saying is that he is not the man she wants. He's too distant. He won't engage in conversation. He doesn't try to emotionally connect with her. He doesn't understand her. I could go on, but you get the point—if he were like I want him to be our "differences" would be resolved and I wouldn't have been unfaithful.

Now, the second one is a little more touchy. There is no doubt that when someone grows up with domestic violence in their home, people will be affected. And, certainly, when someone is opened up to sexuality at an early age, whether being touched inappropriately or seeing it inadvertently, that this will have an effect as well. However, does everyone who has grown up in this environment end up being unfaithful before, during, and after marriage? No. The fact that she could not and would not take sole responsibility was a problem. It felt like it was a bad seed and it sure was.

For the next several months, they spent a lot of time reading their bibles together, reading books that I assigned them to read, and watching videos I assigned them to watch. They swallowed up whatever I gave them. They began praying together and to top it all off, I got them, well the Lord got them, to get rid of Facebook. And, we did some great work uncovering some of the idolatrous desires that were dominating their hearts.

He learned that he desperately wanted a peaceful relationship. For him, that means, they never argue. To her, that means they never talk. You get what I mean? He just wants to work, come home to a quiet home, put his kids to bed, watch TV and go back to work the next morning. She however, wants romance, which means communication, which is exactly what he is not looking for. Well, romance, yes, if you call sex without communication, romance.

When he didn't get his peace, he felt alone, and went to porn. When she didn't get her romance, she became discontent, critical, angry and short-tempered. He then became more distant and the cycle continued until for her, she started looking elsewhere for someone else who would make her feel more loved and more secure.

They hung in there for a while. They spent a ton of time talking, which was painful for him but delightful for her. During their times, though, more lies on her part came out and she began looking for jobs, including ones out of state. He took this as a desire on her part to leave the marriage, which she of course denied, and which of course, he was right. Even though progress was being made, she was on her way out again. Some girls are runners, and she was one of them.

She began building reasons into her mind about how good it would be to move back where they were from. She could get a job there easier. Her family was there. They didn't like California anyway. They could get out of their home here and buy a bigger one there. Her husband, being a weak leader and terrible decision maker and her being a great salesman, she pretty much had him sold on the idea and he turned out to be dead right about her.

Pam did in fact move back and they did in fact end up in divorce. Sad to say, when she went back, she was unfaithful again. This poor guy would never be able to satisfy his wife. I'm not sure any man could. He took it hard and so did I. I thought we were making some progress.

They read all the right books, picked up a ton of great tools for communication, and learned all the lessons but something was never quite right. It bothered me for several years. Then, one day, out of nowhere, Brian invited me out to breakfast. He thought I should know that during the entire time of our counseling, the two of them had been drinking to excess every night. That explained everything. Ugh! So much wasted time. Did they really not think that I should know that?!

The principles

Principle one, people don't tell you everything you need to know. They will even make a pact with each other before they come in for counseling as to what they will not tell me. I could hear Brian and Pam now, "Ok, so we're not going to tell him about our drinking, right? I mean, it's not that big of a deal and we could stop anytime. And, it doesn't really have anything to do with our problems anyway."

I know. You think that's crazy, right? Well, you're right. It is but it also isn't. Counselees do it all the time and so do you. It's in our nature to hide. Consider Adam and Eve in the garden after they had sinned. "Then the Lord God called to the man, and said to him, "Where are you?" And he said, "I heard the sound of Thee in the garden, and I was afraid because I was naked; so I hid myself." There it is. "I hid myself." This is what people do. Fear and shame drive us to secrecy, and with it, like cancer before it is exposed to the light of an MRI, sin grows until it has consumed the body and killed it.

Principle two, there will be times when you meet with people, teaching them all that should be taught. Week after week, you will encourage them, comfort them, exhort them even, and you will not see change. In the back of your mind, you'll wonder, *something's wrong here*. These are good people. They love the Lord. They do all the homework. But week after week, they come back no better than they were before. If you see this, something is wrong. Trust your instincts.

How this can help your ministry

When you get into a situation like this, trust your instincts and ask them a few questions. Ask them why they think they're not changing. Ask them if there is something else going on that they are not telling you. Ask them if they made a pact about what they will or will not tell you. Give them a chance to lie right to your face . . . again. God will take it from there. By the way, you'll often note that one of them is not comfortable with the lie and it will start to come out.

This can be done privately or separately. By that, I mean you can ask them together or you can separate them and ask them individually. Don't tell them before they get to your meeting or they will be onto you and their fears will drive them to further hide. I know it sounds like an ambush, and maybe it is, but it's for their benefit. Sin loves to hide. Without open and honest confession, your counseling will fail and their relationship will fail along with it. Counselors, beg them to be open with you. If you're a pastor, pull your pastor card out and plead with them to be open and honest with you.

One last thing, that you will hear from me again and again: as a counselor and a pastor, I have very few positive things to say about social media, particularly Facebook, Instagram, and snapchat. Get your people off social media!

Steve Mawhorter

Lessons Learned

Chapter 7

Timing is everything

Meet Tim and Sara

Tim and Sara grew up in the church and professed Christ, but if they were believers, they were baby ones at best. They were college grads with good jobs. This was Tim's first marriage but Sara's second. By the time they got to me, they'd been separated for a month.

They had a ton of issues. They were in debt up to their eyeballs and could not agree on how to budget. Though they said church was a priority, they did not have a home church that they could both agree on. One wanted to move. The other didn't. Neither reported being in the Word on any regular basis, which means they hardly ever read it. They prayed occasionally, though never together, which meant they hardly ever prayed. They had no fellowship with other believers. And, readers, that is just the tip of the iceberg.

Both felt unloved and disrespected, even *small* if you will. He was a prideful, angry man with a ton of insecurities. She was physically abused in her first marriage and expected Tim to be more gentle with her than he was, especially since he knew all that she went through in that first marriage. And, she expected him to be a much better spiritual leader than he was, a common cry from women. They had a blended family with children from her first marriage. One of those kids was on drugs. Sara didn't get any child support, so finances were tight as well. If you're wondering about sex, forget it. It wasn't happening. With all of this, you can imagine that there is a lot of bitterness between them, very little forgiveness and very little hope, especially for Sara. Yet, neither wanted out of the marriage.

With what little hope they had, we proceeded. It became apparent that neither one of them were fully aware of how much they had hurt the other or how. They just didn't see it. These guys were in need of a total restructure of life but wow, where do you begin, right? What issue do you start with? In this case, I didn't start with any of those because there was one more piece of information that I haven't told you yet.

On his counseling request form, I noticed that when he was young, he was betrayed by his youth leader. I also noticed that he struggled with his previous boss, which gave him the impetus to leave that business. And, now, he's having trouble finding a church where he trusts the pastor. Do see a pattern here? I did. Tim's got a problem with authority and oh, by the way, I'm an authority in his life now. *Will he have a problem with me, too?* At the same time, I thought to myself, *"when do I deal with this one?" Is that the first one or the second or is that down the road?*

I actually felt like this was going to be the tipping point in the relationship and that if he could reconcile what happened there, and get rid of that bitterness, he could get rid of it here in the marriage as well. But I also noted that he was a very prideful man. I believe if I were to have jumped on that issue right off the bat, he would have not come back. So, I waited for what I thought would be the right time.

That time came around our fourth meeting or so and he's actually the one who brought it up. By this time, he had been back in the Word, back in church (even though they weren't settled on that being their church), and he was doing some of the reading homework I had given him. Through all of that, God was touching his soul. His pride was softening. He was actually admitting his own wrongdoing in those relationships where he was bitter. At the end of the day, he realized that it was his desire for respect that led to his bitterness. Sara's lack of respect for Tim, had picked a major scab in his life and God was trying to heal that so that the marriage could heal.

The principles

First, and as the chapter is titled, *Timing is everything*. It is. I would have lost him had I not given us time to trust each other. I needed him to know I respected him and actually liked him. We had to build a relationship of mutual trust and respect. That took time. Had I jumped on him too quickly, he would have packaged me as just another man abusing his authority over him. He would have been up and out of there very quickly. In fact, he later told me that if I had brought up that topic in the first meeting, he would not have come back.

So, when you meet people, you will see a ton of issues that need to be addressed but address the ones they can handle first. Grab the low-hanging fruit as they say. His pride was not low-hanging. Getting him to read a book and his bible? Now that was low hanging.

Be patient with people. Let them warm up to you. See if the following illustration helps you understand what I mean.

Most people are either beach people or mountain people. I'm a beach guy. There are two ways to get into the ocean. One, you make a run for it. Two, you wade in slowly to see if your body can acclimate to the temperature in the ocean. I'm a run for it guy, but when it comes to counseling, I wade in and I think most people that you don't already know, prefer it that way. Take your time. Let them warm up to before you go for the jugular.

The second principle that comes to mind here is the issue of bitterness. These two were bitter at other people before they got married to each other. That should have been dealt with before they got married, but it wasn't.

How this will help your ministry

We have a premarital counseling ministry at our church. It's been around since the early 90s. We have a 9-week syllabus that we take people through. In it, we cover all the normal premarital counseling topics like the purpose of marriage, the roles of marriage, budgeting, sex and family planning, but we also have 2 weeks on anger and forgiveness. Why? Because every married person I meet with is angry. All of them. They might use a popular, less intrusive synonym like frustrated or upset, but make no mistake. They are angry.

In those chapters on anger and forgiveness, we discuss bitterness and we ask them if they are carrying bitterness towards anyone outside of their relationship with each other. If there is, we spend time on that. I really believe that it is most wise for them to get rid of that bitterness before they get married. Hebrews 12:15 says, "See to it that no one comes short of the grace of God; that no root of bitterness springing up causes trouble, and by it many be defiled." A bitter person getting married may not be bitter at their fiancé now but if they are a bitter person, that bitterness may likely be the Trojan horse that dooms the early years of that marriage. Help them deal with that and then get them married.

Lessons Learned

Chapter 8

Are you the right person?

(Rom. 15:14; 1 Thess. 5:14; Gal. 6:1)

You have lots of friends and one of those friends comes to you for counsel. With respect to your friendship, are you the right person or should someone else handle this one? Great question, huh, and I've been there. To answer that question, I want you to look at both sides and see an example of a negative and a positive ending. Let's start first though, with how the world looks at this.

In an article in Psychology Today, the writer makes a strong case for never counseling someone who is a friend. They consider it unethical and say that it can lead to dangerous situations and even ruin counseling. They say that therapists need to maintain appropriate boundaries between themselves and their counselees or therapy will not work and could potentially be harmful. They call this the frame. Here are the boundaries they follow:

1. No physical contact with a patient.

2. No relationship with a patient outside of the consulting room.

3. The therapist should not treat close relatives or friends of the patient.

4. No practical advice to a patient.

5. Maintain objectivity and neutrality toward the patient and avoid excessive worrying/thinking about the patient.

6. Seek supervision if you are tempted to, and before you do, violate any of these rules.

Other than number 4, to look at this list and dismiss it just because they are coming from *Psychology Today* would be unwise. Wouldn't you agree that we need to be careful about anyone we touch (#1). Wouldn't you agree that seeking supervision if you're tempted would be a good idea (#6)? Of course. Their boundaries are not all bad but they're not all good either. In this chapter, I just want to zero in on numbers 2 (maintaining a relationship outside the counseling room) and 3 (whether it's okay to counsel friends), and 5, which is basically about the issue of bias.

Despite the fact that I have many years of counseling behind me, I have found it difficult to counsel without any bias whatsoever. The fact is, if I already know the person, and I often do, I already have bias. That can be good, but it also can be bad. The point is, there is bias, but does that mean that this bias will get in the way of you being able to objectively hear both sides? I have found that it becomes difficult when you see that there is another side to this person you've known for a long time. And when you see that other side, it can damage the relationship. Here is one personal example that occurred in my first year of counseling.

Meet Clara and Ellen

Clara and Ellen had been friends for years. They were part of small group of very nice Christian women. They had a good thing going. After many years of a difficult marriage, Ellen divorced her husband. It was a tough time for all because they all tried to help Ellen's marriage stay together. As often happens during trying times like these, their friendships bonded.

Ellen eventually re-married a good man. His name was Bob. Sadly, however, within the first week of marriage, the marriage went south. Yeah, you heard that correct, *In the first week!* On the airplane to their honeymoon destination, Ellen got airsick and Bob didn't hold the bag well enough for her and she got mad. Believe it or not, that one silly little event was a seed for the most bitter battle I would ever experience as a counselor for the next 15 years. I've heard worse since. Ugh!

I'd never seen anything like it. Their accounts of events, simple events, were completely opposite. Listen to these:

"You said you'd be home at 5:30." "No, I didn't. I said 5:15."

"You said you'd clean the gutters." "I never said that."

"You didn't even kiss me good night." "I tried." "No, you didn't."
And, on and on it would go.

Boy, could Ellen cry, too. That's another thing I was ill-prepared for. I didn't know people would get that hysterical over leaves and timing. I was in way over my head, but this chapter isn't about me. This one is about my co-counselor, Clara.

Clara and Ellen were best buddies, *bffs* for life as they say. Clara was a new counselor as well. We all thought this would be perfect. Clara and Ellen are best friends. They know each other so well. Clara will have some insight that will be helpful for Bob. I knew Bob a little but not well enough to know what he was really like so I was hoping Clara's pre-relationship with Ellen would be enlightening for him. Sadly, that was not the case.

It was enlightening, but only in the sense that Clara met someone she didn't know, the other side of Ellen, her *bff*. To make a long story short, this counseling relationship went on for 20 meetings in 6 months and it ended bitterly as Ellen left Bob. As a result, the relationship between Clara and Ellen also ended, which also ended the long-term relationships shared by all four women. So sad.

It all sounded like a great idea at first but looking back on it, this was a mistake. It wasn't that Clara had bias that got in the way. In fact, to Clara's credit, she didn't hold back the truth. This woman, her *bff*, was just plain high-high-maintenance. It was a mistake because it blew up their friendship and all those around it. Looking back, maybe if I had a different counselor, the same truth would have been received better by Ellen. Maybe not. Either way, the point of the story is that you may lose friends in the counseling process.

I have plenty of other examples of friends counseling friends and after over 20 years of counseling literally thousands of people, I can say that I have personally only lost one friend this way. Sooner or later, I'll lose another, but does that mean that I should not counsel friends because I lost one? Is the world right about this? Is it unethical? Can it cause more harm than good?

The principle

Counseling can cost you a friendship, period. Yes, it can, but it can also bond other relationships. It can deepen some friendships and destroy others. So, how are we supposed to look at this? For truth, we go to our bibles.

The book of Romans is written to the church in Rome. Do you think they knew each other there? Of course, they did. Romans 15:14 says, "And concerning you, my brethren, I myself also am convinced that you yourselves are full of goodness, filled with all knowledge and able also to admonish one another."

Admonish (noutheteo) means literally "to put into mind," with the purpose of warning and reproving. It is just one aspect of counseling, but according to this passage, we are able to admonish one another and should be. The *one another* in this passage has to include people we know, right?

Ephesians is written to the church in Ephesus. Do you think they knew each other? Of course, they did. Ephesians 4:15 says to speak the truth, one to another. That's not a suggestion. It's a command. Who better to speak the truth in love to another than someone who already knows and loves you?

Galatians is written to the church at Galatia. Do you think they knew each other? Of course, they did. Chapter 6, verse 1 says, "Brethren, even if anyone is caught in any trespass, you who are spiritual, restore such a one in a spirit of gentleness; *each one* looking to yourself, so that you too will not be tempted." Did you catch that first word, *brethren*? We are brothers and sisters in Christ because we are bonded by the blood of Christ and we have the same Father. Brothers are to restore brothers.

1 Thessalonians 5:14 says, "We urge you, brethren, admonish the unruly, encourage the fainthearted, help the weak, be patient with everyone." Did you catch that? Brethren? Yeah, that's all of us. We can and should admonish, encourage, and help each other. The Bible isn't just suggesting that maybe we can counsel those who are our friends. It's commanding it.

And, what about pastors? Can they counsel their sheep or should they farm it out? This will be covered in greater detail in another chapter, but the short answer is yes. Every pastor should be counseling his sheep or he is not being a shepherd. He is an administrator during the week and a speaker on the weekend, but he is not a shepherd unless he is counseling his people.

How this can help your ministry

Counsel each other but be careful about who you counsel. Can you truly hear both sides without bias that would be harmful? Do you already have a negative bias towards either side? If you do, can you truly set that aside and maintain your objectivity? And, what do they believe? Do they believe you are biased? Do they believe you can objectively hear both of them?

And, what about your friendship? Are you willing to lose it. Even if you help them, you still might lose it because they know that you now know things about them that they have been hiding. With this new information, your friendship can either bond or break. Are you ready for either one?

Last, are you the best one to be counseling this person? Your bias could make you the worst, but it could also make you the best. I think I've had it both ways. I have counseled many couples where I knew the wife much better than the husband. I clearly had bias, usually, though not always bias towards the husband or the wife. Just plain bias.

In one particular and typical case, the marriage was on the rocks. She, like any woman, just wanted to feel loved. He hadn't a clue how to do that with her, but I did. So, I helped him grow up as a man, and taught him how to love his wife and win her back, which he did. In this case, my bias actually worked in his favor. Any other male counselor would first have to get to know this man's wife. Would she open up to him? Would she trust that counselor? Would he connect with her? Would she have been willing to wait?

Most of the time, these situations work out well, but the bottom line is, just be careful, thoughtful, prayerful, and count the cost before you begin because you may be the right person but you may also indeed lose a friendship in the process. And, don't listen to Psychology Today to tell you how to help people. Let the Lord do that.

Steve Mawhorter

Lessons Learned

Chapter 9

Swallow hard and tell the truth

(Eph. 4:15)

Meet some counselees

Our world today is obsessed with making people feel good about themselves. Would you agree? Way back in 2005, I googled "self-esteem" to see how many websites would pop up. To my shock and chagrin, 833,000 sites popped up. That's crazy, right? Well, if you do that same google search today, 130,000,000 will pop up! Despite the fact that research has shown that it doesn't work, the world continues to be obsessed with it.

One study that shows its ineffectiveness was done in by Jean Twenge, a professor at San Diego State University. The study followed 16,475 college students from 1982 through 2006. The study concluded this, "efforts to boost self-esteem have not been shown to improve academic performance and may sometimes be counterproductive, the researchers found. Nor does high self-esteem prevent children from smoking, drinking, taking drugs, or engaging in early sex. If anything, high self-esteem fosters experimentation, which may increase early sexual activity and drinking." It doesn't work people. Stop worrying about it.

Now, the purpose of this chapter is not to prove to you that self-esteem is nothing more than narcissism, so I'll leave it there for now. I only bring this up here because this obsession with making people feel good about themselves is keeping us from telling people what we know they need to hear. We're afraid that if we hurt their precious feelings that they will never come back. My hope is that through the following examples, you'll learn to swallow hard and love people enough to tell them the truth.

Meet Sean. Sean was a good, hard-working, faithful guy. But he was an unbeliever. His wife had just confessed her adultery. He wants to know what he should do. What will you tell him? I told him, "put your pride in the trashcan and forgive your wife."

Meet Todd. Another great guy but a guy who had lost just about everything he had. He'd lost his wife due to divorce, a child due to an illness, his job due to the economy, and his friends because he had to move. He asks you why this is all happening to him? What's your answer? My answer was, "this was all God's doing and He's trying to get your attention. So, let's not complain. Let's consider what good God is up to."

Meet Crystal. Crystal was a super sweet girl but also super overweight. She was getting older and her biological clock was ticking away as the child-birthing years were getting away from her. Fearing that she may never marry, she meets a man online. They develop a relationship and want to marry. Great, right? Not great. He's an unbeliever. She wants to know if she can marry him. What will you tell her? I told her, "you can't do that and please God at the same time. The Bible is clear about unequal yoking in marriage." That was a hard one.

Meet hundreds of women whose husbands have just confessed that they have been viewing pornography. What will you tell them? I tell them to forgive him and get him in here. We can help him.

Meet Tonya. Tonya is married to a hard-working guy with his own business, a business that barely makes any money. He wants to not only stick with the business but expand the business. The economy is in the tank and you all agree there is little hope in it getting better. Tonya thinks this is a stupid idea. Privately, you agree. What will you tell her? I told her, "God wants you to trust Him by trusting your husband. Encourage him to go after it and make the best and then we'll all see what God was up to." I also told him, "listen to your wife and if you can't do something in a one-flesh way, don't do it."

Meet Wendy. Wendy's husband was a total jerk. He doesn't work. He doesn't cook. He doesn't clean. He pretends he is going to get rich soon, but he hasn't. He claims to be a believer, but he's left the church and doesn't go to any church now. There are no signs of true faith in him. He takes every penny she makes and buys toys for himself or items that he says he is going to use to make lots of money, which he has never done. She's done, she wants out, and she's asking you if she can divorce him. What will you tell her? I told her, "No. Without sexual immorality, you have no cause. Wait and pray for his repentance."

In chapter 20, "I don't think I can take anymore!," I refer to Harry and Wanda. She'd been molested on two occasions. She was depressed, anorexic, cutting, and so on. You'll see, that after several weeks, we had a super hard session, which amounted to her sobbing in my office for well over an hour. She was in hysterics. I wasn't sure she'd come back the following week, but she did, and she says this to me, "so basically, what you're telling me is that all my problems are due to my own selfishness. Is that correct?" What would you have said? If you said yes, you might end up with another hour-long sob-session, right? If you said no, you're lying because she's right. With a smile, I just shook my head and said, "Yep. You got it." This was the turning point in that counseling relationship.

Ok, one more. Meet Greg. Greg's wife had committed adultery and as you might suspect, he was mad as a hornet. He couldn't believe she could do such a thing. His pride was so glaring that I had to say something that I hate saying even though I know it's true. Here's what I told him.

"Though I know many men who have committed adultery even though they had wives who loved and respected them, I do not know any women who felt loved by their husbands and yet still committed adultery. Zero. Nada. Not one. I'm sure there is someone out there who has, but I've never met her." I continued, "Greg, she needs to take responsibility for her sin. She did it out of her own selfishness. No one made her do it. She did it on her own, period. But, you my brother, you need to take responsibility for making her vulnerable to such a thing. Married, Christian women do not naturally do this like men do." Yikes, that was hard to say. But you know what, it turned the counseling around. Now, he could focus on his own sin instead of hers.

Please know that in all of these examples, I said a lot more than the one or two sentences in this book. My comments were always in love, gentle, careful, and with compassion, fashioned around a good relationship between me and the counselees.

The principle

You may all find this hard to believe, but to my knowledge, I have never had someone not come back for my counseling (in just the initial meeting) because I told them something that they didn't like or want to hear. I'm sure there is someone out there that I am not aware of who didn't, but I am aware of hundreds who specifically come to me *because* they expect me to tell them the truth whether they like it or not. Are you finding that hard to believe?

I have found that most Christians are like the old toy called, "the Bozo the clown inflatable punching bag." Remember that? You could punch it as hard as you wanted and it would go down to the ground and then pop right back up. People who love God and the Word are like that. You can hit 'em hard with truth and they'll come back for more. But, why?

Eph. 4:15, tell us, "speak the truth in love," and people want the truth. So, in a loving way and out of love for the person, you swallow hard and tell them the truth. Watch and see if they push away from you or move towards you.

How this can help your ministry

Being known as someone who will tell you the truth in a loving way and out of love for them will build trust in your people. More people will come because this is what they want in the first place. One of the all-time great movie lines is from the movie, *A Few Good Men* with Jack Nicholson and Tom Cruise. Cruise's character demands the truth. Nicholson's character responds, "you can't handle the truth." Folks, it makes for a great line in a movie but it's a lie in real life. People want someone to tell them the truth. Give it to them. They can handle it.

If you let fear rule your counseling, you'll never really help anyone. Yes, people need to be encouraged and comforted and they need your patience and steadfastness. They want to be loved, right? Well we know from Scripture that fear and love are opposite ends of the spectrum. What I'm saying here is, put your fears about how people will react and love your brothers and sisters in Christ by telling them the truth. Our culture has us believing that if we tell people something hard, they won't come back. I just need you to know, that is not true. Our experience is that our people come back. They want the truth, so give it to them and give it to them in a loving way.

Lessons Learned

Chapter 10

What? Me sin? Never

(Eccl. 7:20)

Meet Alex and Barbara

Alex is a successful businessman. He reported that his health was good and that he sleeps well. He noted 2 major events in his life, one being a DUI that he had received 20 years ago, the other being the recent loss of his father. Spiritually, he claims to be saved, and loves learning from solid bible teachers like Dr. MacArthur and Dr. Sproul. He regularly attends church, has regular devotions, and prays before meals and bedtimes with the kids. He says he's never backslid from his faith. He describes himself as active, ambitious, self-confident, persistent, hardworking, imaginative, serious, good-natured, extroverted, likeable, leader, and submissive. When asked what brought him here, he answered, "my wife," an all too common problem. He listed as his biggest issues being spending too much time on the computer and time management, which kind of go together anyway. Sounds pretty good so far, right?

Well, not so fast. What he didn't say is that he smokes, drinks, and has been incredibly, unbelievably, verbally abusive to his sweet wife. To be truthful, his verbal abuse was the worst I had ever seen at that early point of my ministry. How is it that he failed to mention those things on his counseling request form, right?

Barbara had a group of solid Christian friends and was very involved with her children and prayer ministries for them and their school. She grew up in an episcopal church and later a Methodist church, which will turn out to be key as the story develops. She said she was saved as a young girl but had really just reconnected with the Lord and in a much closer way, more than she can ever remember. She says she prays often, attends church regularly, reads her bible occasionally and that the family has regular family devotions. She's active, ambitious, hardworking, blue, imaginative, likeable, leader, dedicated (to her marriage), concerned, calm, frustrated, and a good mother. Sounds good, right? Again, not so fast.

It was super easy to see all of Alex's sins. They were blatant, in your face. He was a raging alcoholic and abusive to his wife and children. He truly was the problem in all this and I needed to go after him but because he was so prideful, too, I needed to address some of her issues as well and I do mean a little. I didn't want to empower him by getting after her too much. So, for their first assignment, I asked them to come up with a list of sins that they commit on a regular basis that has been harming the marriage. He came back with an honest list this time, including his alcoholism and abuse. Barbara came back with nothing, I mean literally, nothing. How is that possible, right?

Well, to say the least, I was a bit shocked. She's a good girl and a rule follower, if you know what I mean. This should have been an easy assignment for her. When I asked her why she didn't do her homework, she said, "*I can't think of any sins I commit.*" Incredulously, I said, "*you never sin?*" She said, "*no.*" And, she meant it.

After taking a second to gather myself, I asked if she ever gets impatient. She said, "why sure, of course." I asked if she ever gets angry. Again, she said, "why sure, of course." By this time, she was getting it and asked, "are those sins?" With great excitement and laughter (both of us), I said yes. She literally exclaimed, "*I didn't know that . . . Well then, I sin a lot!*" We got a big hoot out of that one. This was a turning point for her and really set counseling in a good direction.

The principle

As counselors, pastors, mentors, and friends, it's easy to see other people's sins. They stare us right in the face like a teenager with bad acne. Who could miss that?! If you're like me, you're thinking, "how is it possible that they did not see themselves as sinners?" How could a drunk not know he is a drunk? How could a Christian not know that impatience and anger are sins? Well, some don't.

Lessons Learned

In the July/2015 edition of Chritianity Today, they note the following staggering statistics regarding the biblical illiteracy of Christians today. Here's what they noted, "Christians claim to believe the Bible is God's Word. We claim it's God's divinely inspired, inerrant message to us. Yet despite this, we aren't reading it. A recent LifeWay Research study found only 45 percent of those who regularly attend church read the Bible more than once a week. Over 40 percent of the people attending read their Bible occasionally, maybe once or twice a month. Almost 1 in 5 churchgoers say they *never* read the Bible—essentially the same number who read it every day." From a big picture perspective then, it's not surprising that Barbara didn't see it.

For Barbara, remember her spiritual growing up experience? Her roots were in the Episcopal church and the Methodist church, churches not known for making a big deal out of sin and as she indicated, she wasn't really in the Word all that much. In fact, she would tell me that she thought that only a breakage of the ten commandments was sin and she'd never done those. She literally was just unaware that her impatience and infrequent frustration with Alex was sin.

For Alex, his sin is what blinded him. He didn't realize it, but his alcoholism kept him trapped and unaware. As I look back, it's actually quite possible that he was not saved to begin with. We are known by our fruits, not our works. He did the works; go to church, read your bible, listen to good sermons, don't commit adultery, etc., etc. But, where was the fruit—love, joy, peace, patience, kindness, goodness, etc.? These were absent, drowned out by alcohol.

When each were able to see and admit the sins they were committing, our counseling began to take shape. Barbara was a delight. She committed right away to mend her ways and she did. Alex made that same commitment and for the next 2 months of counseling, he did not drink. Their humility was refreshing and gave me much hope that we could get below the surface of their sins and get to the root causes.

The fact is, they did allow me to dig a little deeper. Like the rest of us, lurking in the shadows of our minds, are those desires that drive us all to sin. Biblical counselors call these "idols of the heart." Barbara learned that her desire for a peaceful marriage, which she could not attain, had led her to angry outbursts, to trying to control Alex, and it began pushing her away from prayer and church attendance with her husband. Alex learned that his desire for personal recognition (pride) had led him down the path of destruction that he was now on. This was very helpful for them.

He quit drinking and she let go of trying to control him. Their priorities changed from pleasing self to pleasing God. Their family times became much sweeter. Her desire for a peaceful marriage was now being met and his desire to feel respected was being returned in kind. Funny how that is.

How this can help your ministry

People don't always know that they are sinning. Some people don't even know that anything beyond "the 10 commandments" can be sin. However, when you show them what they're doing is sin, a believer with God's help, will see it and want to change it. In 1 Kings 8:58, we find newly crowned King Solomon praying to the Lord on behalf of the people. He says, "that He may incline our hearts to Himself, to walk in all His ways to keep His commandments and His statues and His ordinances, which he commanded our fathers."

Solomon's prayer reminds us that it is He that moves our hearts towards Him. He is faithful to do that, but He uses you in people's lives to help them see it. Just show it to them. Stop expecting people to "get it" when it comes to sin. Start expecting them to be unaware and you'll find yourself being more compassionate. 2 Timothy 3:16 starts with teaching and that's where counseling begins. Just teach them and watch God begin to work in their lives.

Lessons Learned

Chapter 11

I swear to God, I didn't do it!

Sometimes, you just know when you're talking with someone that you're not getting the whole story. What do you do? Press in on that and play detective or wait on the Lord?

Meet Tina and Aaron

Tina was one of those women you like the instant you meet her. Back in my day, we would call her a yuppie, a young urban professional. She's got it all going on. Tina's attractive; she has a good sense of humor, and she smiles a lot. With her engaging personality, she could be so convincing that she could probably sell ice to an Eskimo. Tina had a great career, a hard-working husband, and good children.

Tina had grown up in the church but as many kids do once they're out of the home, she fell away from the Lord, and married an unbeliever. This is a super common story I hear—Christian women marrying non-Christian men. Why do I not hear or see Christian men marrying non-Christian women? That's odd when you consider that in the Bible, you see that Jewish men falling to unbelieving gentile women was their weakness. Think Samson, David, Solomon. That list could go on. In any case, this is what Tina did. She married an unbelieving, hard to please man.

Without question, her desire to please her husband proved to be an idol in her life. She tried all 5 of the love languages; gifts, acts of service, words of affirmation, quality time and quality touch. None of it worked. He was impossible to please. But this was her choice and she needed to make the best of.

Well, I got a call one evening from a friend who said that one of his friends was convinced that his wife, Tina, was having an affair and, as you might imagine, he was infuriated about it. My friend wanted me to meet with him, so I did. Aaron was exactly what my friend said, convinced and infuriated. We met for 2 hours that night. He was doing some real soul searching. He asked me to meet with Tina and so Tina and I met the very next morning.

I had never met Tina before, and our meeting was delightful. We also met for two hours. Right away, she said, "I swear to God. I didn't do it." She ensured me that her husband was out of his mind, that she did not have an affair. I didn't know her at all until this day, and even though I suspected she might not be telling me the whole truth yet, I accepted her words and then began listening to her testimony.

As she was sharing her testimony, she could tell that I wasn't a bad guy and that I was there to care for her. I'm pretty sure she felt safe with me and that she could trust me. So, about thirty minutes into her story, as she was reminded of the roots of childhood faith, she admitted that she had indeed kissed a man, but that it was only one time. Again, I accepted her words but suspected there might be a little more than that.

She continued to talk, and I continued to listen. The more she talked, the more comfortable she felt, and the more the Holy Spirit reminded her of who she was – a believer. So, she came clean and confessed that she had indeed had intercourse with a man, but it was only one time. Again, I accepted her words but suspected there might be a little more than that. I just let her talk and let the Holy Spirit do the rest. And, He did.

After about ninety minutes of this, she came clean with the rest. It was of course more than once. It was an affair. She felt foolish. She felt shame. Some tears finally came out. I think her words were something like, "I was so stupid!" Which is true. She was stupid. Aren't we all?! More importantly, she was confessing, and I was responding in a loving way.

Tina's confession and contrition made it easy for me to respond with grace and mercy. She had married an unbeliever, who in her mind, did not love her, and who was impossible to please. These are key issues for women. Every woman wants to feel loved. And, all women desire to please their husbands; well, at least in the early years they do. Sadly, as these desires were not fulfilled, they became idolatrous and she became vulnerable. She was an accident waiting to happen and it did.

Lessons Learned

Before I get to the principles in this story, you probably want to know how this one turned out. Well, it turned out well. To keep it brief, she repented and turned back to Christ. Her husband, an unbeliever at the time, came to faith, and their marriage continues to strengthen to this day. Now, to the principles.

The principles

There are two that I want to touch on. One, though not related to the title of this chapter, is a very important lesson. Any woman who feels unloved by her husband is vulnerable to sexual sin. As I write that, many women reading this chapter will think to themselves, "I would never do that!" Listen, you're kidding yourself and underestimating the power of sin and the weakness of your flesh (Matt. 16:41).

You are human. So am I. You know as a woman that sex brings you pleasure and makes you feel loved. Science has taught us this. We actually know and have named the chemicals that are released during the sexual act. Your body is designed this way by God. But, God also designed us in such a way that sex will not only give you pleasure but will make you feel you are loved and in love, even though that feeling may only last a few minutes. Don't kid yourself. Be on guard for yourselves.

And, if you're a man reading this chapter, do yourself and your wife a favor. Protect her from vulnerability and love that woman. If she doesn't feel loved, humble yourself and figure out why. You'll save yourself and your wife from the misery that comes from unfaithfulness.

Second, and related to the title of this chapter, people will rarely tell you the whole truth right off the bat. Tina knew who I was but only in name and that I was the head of the biblical counseling ministry at a large church. Why would she tell me something that might get back to her husband and blow up her family? So, of course she would swear she didn't do it. Don't expect people to confess something to you when they barely know you. Give it time.

Counselors and pastors, you can trust God with the truth. As I've already written, it will come out (chapter 2). It always does, sooner or later. It doesn't have to be your timing. You don't have to badger someone into confession. Just love them. Care for them. If they trust you will handle them with care, they will begin to open up. And, the more gracious you are with your response, the more open they will be with you. Let me illustrate that for you in the next section.

How this can help your ministry

You might be familiar with what we call the roly-poly bug. You might know it as the pill bug. It's that bug in your garden that curls up into a ball as soon as you touch it. This is what people do when they do not feel safe with you. They curl up and hide. They'll swear on the Bible, even while totally lying right to your face, until they feel safe with you. And, they'll feel safe with you if they feel loved by you.

The bottom line here is, don't expect people who barely know you to tell you the truth, the whole truth, and nothing but the truth. Let it come out on its own and love them when they confess.

Lessons Learned

Chapter 12

Tear up those papers

(Lk. 9:62)

Meet Chad and Maria and Ron and Kimberly

Chad and Maria were Christians at a good church. Maria was a regular attender, involved in a bible study, and had a few good friends, though not many.

Chad was also an attender, but an irregular one at best. He didn't attend any bible studies, didn't serve anywhere, and was basically unknown to his church body.

By the time they got to us, the husband had already filed for divorce. He was not only done; he was done-done, if you know what I mean. Still, even though their marriage had a mountain of problems to overcome, I felt that due to their stated beliefs and their open honesty with each other, that we could make up some ground, and maybe save the marriage.

For that to happen, though, this would take a full and total surrender of every area of their lives. She would need to walk away from alcohol, anger, verbal abuse, discontentment and so on and so on. He, by his own admission would have to learn what it means to love his wife, the church, and the Lord. He would later write that they have never had a Christian marriage. He was right. I could not find one thing about their marriage that looked Christian. So sad.

Well, for them to make any of this happen, they would have to recommit to the marriage. She was willing and after meeting with me a few times, he was as well, though he had one foot in and one foot out of the door. To gain a commitment, I wanted his divorce papers. I figured that if I could get him to give me those, then we would have both of those feet in the door. And, guess what. He did, and counseling began.

To be sure, the beginning of counseling was rough. They didn't get where they were overnight. It was going to take a long time. Sadly, Chad did not have enough patience for this. One night, they had a big fight and he came in the next morning, demanding I give him back the divorce papers. To my shame, instead of shredding them when he gave them to me, I had placed them in his file. So, I gave them to him and that was the end of that.

The story illustrates that I never really had a commitment from him in the first place, which is paramount to the success of marriage counseling. Their marriage ended months later.

Meet Ron and Kimberly. I loved these two. They were solid citizen people who loved the Lord. They had several kids, who were all delightful. They attended a good church and were very involved there.

These two were college sweethearts who remained pure throughout their dating relationship and into their marriage. They were the perfect couple, that is, until the beast of pornography snuck into the marriage.

His job required him to be away from his wife for long stretches, even overnight at times. This is often a recipe for disaster and in this case, it was. He began looking at pornography. This lasted for years.

Thankfully, and on his own, he repented and stayed away from it for many years. Then, one day, he felt convicted about his past and confessed it to his wife. This did not go over very well. In fact, it picked a major scab in their marriage. You see, Ron had lied about a physical relationship he had with another woman before they were married. He had told her nothing ever *happened*, also a lie. This was the beginning of all their troubles.

Kimberly always wanted to marry a man who had been with no woman but her. She thought she'd found that in Ron. When he told her the truth about that relationship, she felt tricked by God, which on a human level, is understandable. Coupled with this revelation and the revelation about pornography, she was hurt, massively hurt.

I want to be clear here. These were lovely people, the kind you would want to be your best friends, the kind of people that you would trust your own kids with. But this was too much for her to handle. She couldn't sleep, struggled with fear, couldn't focus on her children, and had little to no sexual interest. She complained and grumbled, indulged her flesh, carried a great deal of unforgiveness and really struggled with the sovereignty of God. "How could He let this happen to me when I've been so good?"

After meeting for about 6 months, Kimberly wanted out of the marriage. Well, not really. She didn't want out. She wanted out of her misery. Who could blame her? She would bathe in his sin all day, every day, from the time she woke up until the time she went to bed. This desire to be with a man who was always pure was her idol and she worshipped it well. It was sad to watch.

We got to the point where I needed to know if she was all-in or if she wanted out of the marriage, so I gave her a paper to read on the "Providence of God – does God cause evil?" I asked her to read that paper and to come back with a 1 page, front and back, paper of her own, summarizing what she'd read and to tell me whether she was in or if she was out. If she was out, we would be done with counseling. Yikes, this one was scary.

Again, I really loved this couple. It was so sad to see her locked up by her own pride and unforgiveness. And this man, Ron, was solid. He'd be a candidate for elder at your church. Yeah, he's that good. She ought to meet a bunch of the other men I've met with over the years. She'd be more thankful . . . maybe. Actually, I doubt it. She was stubborn and stuck. So, I made her make a decision.

Well, she came the following week, fully committed to the marriage and our counseling went on from there. Progress was made. I haven't seen them in years. I miss them, both of them.

The principle

Counseling will not go anywhere until you have a commitment from both sides that they are all-in no matter what. If either one of them has one foot in and one foot out like Chad, counseling will go nowhere. But, if you can get both of them to have both feet in like Ron and Kimberly, it may take some time, buy you'll get there.

How this can help your ministry

It should be obvious but in case it's not, you need to develop a plan for gaining a commitment to the marriage. This can be done in a few ways.

One, you just assume you have it unless you see later that you may not. Two, you can straight up ask for it. Ask them what they want. Do they want to stay married no matter what or are they open to divorce if "this" doesn't work?

Jesus illustrates this point when, "By the pool of Bethesda, lay several who were sick, blind, lame, and withered. One man was ill for thirty-eight years. Jesus, knowing he had been that way for a long time, asked the man, "do you want to get well?" (John 5:1-6). It's a simple question but one we can and often should ask. There are many advantages to gaining this type of commitment, both to the counselor and the counselee.

To the counselor, among others, it sets a pattern for change, places the responsibility on the counseling, generates hope, sustains momentum, and keeps the focus on the solution. To the counselee, it decreases dependence on the counselor, becomes a benchmark for the future, and because they are growing, their confidence in Scripture will increase.

Last, I want to encourage you to not be afraid to call someone out for not being committed. Don't waste your time and their time if either one of them is on the fence. Pee or get off the pot is the way the world puts it. Crude, but it says it well. Biblically, you're either with me or against Me. Make a decision.

In Luke 9, Jesus addresses a group of followers who were sure they would follow Him wherever He would go. They said they were ready to follow but just needed to wait until their parents died first, then they could go. Jesus knew they weren't really committed and said to them, "No one, after putting his hand to the plow and looking back, is fit for the kingdom of God (Lk. 9:62)." If you want to move forward with the Lord, there's no looking back. You're all in or you're out. Show them the passage and ask them if they are ready for this.

Lessons Learned

Chapter 13

Put those labels where they belong

(2 Tim. 3:16-17)

Meet Eric

Eric was one of those clean-cut, never did anything seriously wrong kind of guys. He grew up in a nominally Catholic home, but Catholicism never really landed in his heart. Sometime during his college years, he was invited to an evangelistic event and it was there he thought he had received the Lord. Shortly after, he met a girl while attending a church, they got married and had kids. End of story, right? Not so fast.

After 10 years of marriage, while attending a good bible teaching church, Eric's wife filed for divorce without cause. As you can imagine, he was shocked, but she was immovable. The church met with them one time but, seeing her immovability, they dropped the ball from there. Sadly, the marriage ended.

Five or so years later, when Eric came to me, I saw him as a guy who loved the Lord, loved the Word, loved his church, and loved to worship. He even served on the worship team at his church.

Eric had a good enough job to support he and his children, but due to some troubles he was having with some of his co-workers, his employment had instructed him to seek some help. However, the help he got was not much help at all.

By the time he got to me, he had been diagnosed with Obsessive Compulsive Personality Disorder (OCPD). According to psychologists, OCPD is a personality disorder that is characterized by extreme perfectionism, order, and neatness. People with OCPD will also feel a severe need to impose their own standards on their outside environment.

The description of that label fit Eric to a tee. When he came in, he rated his troubles with anger and anxiety and worry as a 7 on a scale of 1-10. And, he rated perfectionism as a 10. He reported that he even quit a job one time due to the stress over things he was not able to control. He was also rigid and controlling. What he was hoping to get from me was some good stress and anxiety coping mechanisms, something which the psychologist said would help him with his *disorder*.

Again, if anyone actually *had* OCPD (if you buy that as something you can *have*), Eric was it, but even though he appeared to have this disorder, he himself was struggling to accept the label. Something inside him was not quite ready to believe this. In my opinion, that's really why he came to me. I think he knew that I would not be into the psychological labels heaped on us by unbelieving people but would instead speak truth to him, which he loved and wanted. So, in love and compassion, I gave it to him.

We started by just letting go of the label for now. I told him, "let's just address a few other things first and then we'll see what you think about the label." We started with two things that I thought were really central to all of this. One was simple. The other more complicated.

The more complicated item was the providence of God. We spent two weeks on that subject. I asked him to read a chapter out of Wayne Grudem's *Systematic Theology* on the providence of God. And, I asked him to memorize and meditate on Philippians 2:3-4. I assigned these two because I believe that his main problems were that he needed to learn to trust God in the everyday issues of life and because he is very self-focused. Additionally, I asked him to speak to his children and possibly his ex-wife, who he had good communication with, to make a list of sin issues. I figured that if anyone knows our issues, it's our family.

As you might expect, Eric came back with all of his homework done and he found it very valuable. His family reported to him that he was selfish, discontent, inflexible, and angry. They saw him as a person without joy and wallowing in self-pity. Ouch, right?! Yeah, but Eric ate that up.

This is what he wanted. He wanted someone to tell him the truth, not make a label out of him. His family was right, and he was thankful that they loved him enough to tell him the truth. In the weeks ahead, we would address those but in addition, and more importantly, we needed to get down to idolatry, the easier item. What desire was in his heart that was so strong that he would sin if he did not get it or he would sin to get it?

I started by assigning the usual passages that I go to when using the Fruit Tree Illustration, that being James 1:14-15, Mark 7:20-24, Ezekiel 14:1-11, Eph. 4:1-3, Col. 3:12-14, 1 Cor. 13:4-7. I assigned those for him to read and meditate on. He of course (true to his diagnosis) did his homework and we had another great session.

He came back in full agreement that he was harsh, impatient, rigid, and angry when things don't go his way. He agreed that he gets gloomy easy because he is discontent, feeling like everyone else is more gifted than he is. At the end of our meeting, he agreed that what he really, really wants is for everything to go smoothly and in order. This is where the providence of God comes in.

For Eric, anything that got in the way of his idol (wanting everything to go smoothly) would make him angry. This would include traffic, a fellow employee breaking his concentration or making his job harder, his kids wearing certain clothes or even the practice session at church lingering later while everyone is goofing off. Anything that didn't go smoothly would make him mad, which at the end of the day was his main problem. But what or who is he really mad at? That's the problem.

If you understand the providence of God, then you know who and what he was mad at. It was God. You see, the providence of God says that everything that comes your way (traffic, etc.), everything comes *from* Him. Yes, *from* Him. God brought the traffic. God gave him those difficult employees. God made sure the worship practice would be out of order and almost a waste of time. Those things don't just happen. God orchestrates all things for our good and His glory (Rom. 8:28-29).

Between the video I gave him and the assignment from Grudem's book, Eric totally got this and it changed his life. He realized he was angry at God and needed to trust God with those things, embrace them as coming from His wise and loving hand, and then to deal with it biblically.

He realized he needed to love those people by being patient and gentle with them. He needed to learn to go with God's flow as He brought it.

Within only 5 or 6 weeks, Eric had learned why he was the way he was and how to change that. He learned that even though the label he was given,

OCPD, fit, it did not have to be his ongoing identity. In fact, his identity is really in Christ. He is a Christian who struggles with selfishness and trusting God. Well, what do you know, he's just like all the rest of us, isn't he? As Eric and I concluded, He left confident and fired up to go out there and love people.

The principles

I learned a couple of things with Eric. One, I learned that people who love God, His Word, and His church can grow very quickly especially when they are as humble and teachable as Eric was. All I had to do was instruct his heart and give it time (2 Tim. 3:16-17).

Two, I learned that some people don't like the labels and when they are willing to see themselves biblically, they can change rapidly. Eric didn't believe the label and knew it was wrong. He knew his problem was sin. He just didn't know how to address it. Getting to his desires that were ruling his life and causing the sin was the key.

How this can help your ministry

Don't be fooled by the labels and don't feel like you have to fight with your counselees over the accuracy of the label. Just take the symptoms as they are presented and deal with them from a biblical perspective. Help them get to the root of the problem, which is not the sin you see but the desires beneath. Again, what do they want so bad that they are willing to sin to get it or they sin if they don't get it?

I highly recommend you look into the various forms of the Fruit Tree illustration put out there by biblical counselors. CCEF does one that is very intricate. In his book, *Gospel Treason*, Brad Bigney explains a simpler one. And, you can always contact us at NorthCreek Church for an even easier one. It doesn't have to be complicated, people. Keep it simple.

In our church, I am famous for many things, but the most popular saying is probably this, "We want what we want when we want it the way we want it. And, when we don't get it, we get …." Just help people figure out what they want that they don't have, or what they have but they don't want, and you are well on your way to being a major help in someone's life.

Lessons Learned
Chapter 14

Start with him

(Ruth 2:4-17)

Meet Bob and Betty

Betty comes in for counseling with her husband, Bob. She's frustrated, hurt, lonely, discouraged, and tired. That's most women that come in for counseling. Bob tells you that he can't figure out what's wrong. He works hard, they have a home, and they have good friends at their church. "Nothing is ever enough," he tells you. She looks at what they have and wonders if she's going crazy because it's not enough for her. "Maybe, I'm what they call high maintenance?" So, who's right? Is she high maintenance or is he a lazy husband? And, how are you going to handle this one? Will you start with her or him?

Before I get into the principles, I just want to say that this situation is all too common. That's why there isn't more to the *Bob and Betty* in this story. This is very much the norm. Dissatisfied wives bringing in lazy husbands. I hate to denigrate my own gender but people, it is what it is. Rather than argue it out, let's just own it and fix it.

The principles

The purpose of this book is to bring to you something that is not specifically taught in the Scriptures but is learned by the experience of counseling thousands of people over a 40-year time frame, mostly in the last 2 decades. One of those things I've learned over time is that when you have a married couple in the room, you need to press the man first. Now, what do I mean by that?

Well, we know that it takes two to tango per se but in that tango, there is one leader. As the leader goes, so goes the dance. In a marriage, as the leader goes, so goes the marriage and that leader is the man. If they're in your office for counseling, I know that both of them have issues, but I also have learned that the man has very likely led them into that trouble. Always? No. Usually? Yes.

This does not excuse her at all. You've probably seen the T-shirt that says "I'm with stupid" and has a finger pointing to their right or left, presumably the person who is stupid. Only women are allowed to buy and wear these T-shirts, right? Well, sometimes a woman shows up with her version of *stupid* (that's her husband) and is hoping you will fix him. But most of the time, I have found that women know that they, too, have issues. They know and they expect you to instruct her but what they really want to know from you is, will you deal with his sin because even though she is aware of her issues, he is not necessarily aware of his. This chapter is written to encourage you to start with him, not her.

Now, before I go on, I need to outline several advantages in starting with the husband. First, if you go after both at the same time, you may very well empower his dominance. Men usually think it's the woman's fault. So, when you go after her, he's thinking, *yes, he* (that's you, counselor) *gets it.* He thinks you're on his team. And, what do you think she's thinking?

That's right. You *are* on his team. She's thinking *oh, brother. Here we go again. It's all my fault.* You see, now she's not only up against her husband and his authority. Now, she's up against his AND yours. Folks, that's a lot of testosterone to battle. This is, by the way, another reason why it's a good idea to have a female counselor with you. She can help you balance that out.

Second, you need to win her trust. She already doesn't trust her husband and usually for good reason. She's coming to you now to see if you will believe her. Will you? If you don't, you'll squash her spirit. Counseling will probably not last long and not much will change. You will not win her by making her feel, in front of him, that fault lies equally with both. I know, I can hear you thinking, *what if it is equally her fault?*

Okay, what if? It doesn't matter. He is the leader. He is the head of his household. We believe that, right? Then, fix the head and *then* see if the body (her) still needs fixing. She might and I have had a few of those. Bitterness may have already set in but that's okay. You'll deal with that as you go.

Third, how do you think they got married in the first place? Most likely, he pursued and won her over. Then, as so many men do, they take their trophy and put it on the shelf to look at. In some cases, they just put it in a box in the closet and open it every now and then when they want to have sex, which by the way, is a terrible barometer for how the marriage is doing.

Last, men are born to initiate. We look to the Scriptures and find numerous examples. We see Jacob, being forced and tricked into marrying her not-so-good looking sister, Leah, first and having to wait 14 years for his real love, Rachel. We see Solomon's depiction of the man pursuing his love and then her responding to it. Boaz and Ruth are a classic example in my book. If you read it carefully, Ruth was working in the field and Boaz "noticed" her. The next thing you know, drawn like magnet, he moves into her life (Ruth 2:4-17).

You can also find evidence in the creation order from Genesis 2, Eph. 5, and 1 Cor. 11. When men respond to the call to love their wives, and women respond with their call to respect, marriage is not really very difficult.

That's pretty good evidence for the importance of a man pursuing his wife but I'm not calling on that alone. I'm asking you to listen to my experience on this one as well. So, listen up: I have had men who lived with a respectful wife and still left her for another woman, but I have yet to have one woman who felt loved by her husband and has still left him for another man. I'm sure some counselor or pastor has, but I have not.

How this can help your ministry

I used to feel insecure about getting after one spouse and not the other. I no longer do. I have learned that if I can get him to learn how to love his wife, she will fall into place just fine. That does not mean I ignore her issues. In fact, my first assignment will be to ask each of them to come up with ways that they have harmed the marriage on a consistent basis.

When they come back, I won't ignore hers, but I will camp on his. I want him to know that the marriage is in trouble because his wife does not feel loved. And, when she does, the marriage will be much better. I want him to hear that and I want her to hear me say that.

As I look over my years of counseling and all the people I've counseled, it amazes me how many men will not get this. I give them an easy formula, one with guarantees, yet their pride will not allow them to bow their knee to the throne of grace and love their wives. How plainly can the Scripture make it for us, guys, "So husbands ought also to love their own wives as their own bodies. He who loves his own wife loves himself" (Eph. 5:28). The bottom line is, start with the guys and see where that takes you.

Lessons Learned

Chapter 15

I only do it once in a while

(Deuteronomy 30:15)

All addicts lie and manipulate. Look at these lines I've heard and see if you've ever heard these before:

- "I only use on occasion."
- "I'll never do that again."
- "I used to be addicted, but now I can limit myself to just one drink."
- "I have it under control."
- "I can stop anytime I want."
- "You are just jealous because I can have fun and you can't."
- "You never want me to enjoy myself."
- "It's your fault I'm this way."
- "You don't even try to understand how I feel."
- "You wouldn't say that if you loved me."

If you've heard these, then you probably have an addict close to you either as a child, parent, spouse, or counselee. Having someone lie to you hurts, doesn't it? The promises you hear: the promise to do better, to go to meetings, to start going to church, to get another job, to see a counselor, to go to AA or NA, and the promises to change friendships. The promises are endless, and even though they may believe them at the time, they are still lies. The breakage of trust from lying is the worst part of the whole thing.

Where there is no trust, there is no relationship, and no hope. To be betrayed by a loved one, is one of the deepest pains anyone can feel. Your addict husband, child, friend, or counselee, has wounded you so deeply for so long, that you yourself can lose hope in him/her ever changing. For those of you going through this, I feel for you. There is no quick or easy answer to this problem for you, but having a little experience with users, maybe I can shed a little light on this and maybe that will help you as you navigate through these trying times.

Meet addicts

I think the first thing we all need to do when counseling anyone is understand the problem. How can a person lie like this without seemingly any remorse? What possesses a person to lie right to your face? Well, for an addict, or for anyone else for that matter, there can be many reasons. I'll name a few in no particular order.

First, addicts are stubborn people. They've decided they like the path they are on and don't want to change. Sounds crazy, right? They'll lose their family, their job, their friendships, everything, just so they can use?! Yep, you wouldn't believe how many people I've had in my office who just plainly say, "I love being high." They love the escape. Their fantasy world is much more exciting (and easy) than anything real. To them, it's a slice of heaven. Who wouldn't want that? That's crazy thinking, but it's what they think and so, they lie to you so that you don't take that away from them.

Second, they lie to keep loved ones around. They need you to stay around. They need your money. They need to feel like their lies about changing will not cause them to lose you. They need to believe that you'll still be there *when* they quit because they are often convinced that sooner or later, they will.

Third, they lie so that no one will find out. They know what people will think of them and they know that many people will reject them when they find out so lying becomes necessary. In a word, they lie out of fear.

Fourth, they lie to avoid the shame that comes with the truth. The shame of being a user is one thing but the shame from the hurt you've inflicted on others is still another and not easily lost. Shame is a horrible thing and will drive a person to hide just like Adam and Eve. They disappear from people.

If you know someone who hasn't been around much lately, I'll bet you dollars to doughnuts something is going on. It may not be drugs, but something's not right. If someone came to your mind as you're reading this, you should give that person a call.

The principles

There's room for compassion here. I know you're thinking that I'm talking about compassion for you, the victim, and there is compassion for your life experience for sure, but what I'm talking about is compassion for your drug-using, lying, spouse, sibling, child, or counselee. Yes, even they are deserving of compassion and for several reasons.

First, they are trapped. Galations 6:1 says, "Brethren, even if anyone is caught in any trespass, you who are spiritual, restore such a one in a spirit of gentleness; *each one* looking to yourself, so that you too will not be tempted." There is much to be gained in this verse but for this paragraph, I want you to note the word *caught*. In plain English, it means trapped, like being trapped in the woods by a bear trap. You cannot get yourself out. Addicts are trapped, folks. Yeah, yeah, they got themselves there but nonetheless, they are there and they are trapped.

Second, addicts, true addicts, not occasional users, need their drugs to function. They need them to get through another day. They need them to keep from getting sick. They need them to work, to sleep, to get through the next meeting. They need them so they don't have to face what they know is coming, the eventual shame that will accompany the eventual confession. Can you see why they *need* them?

Drugs are incredibly powerful. No one knows the power of these drugs other than a former user. It would greatly help your counseling ministry if you had someone on your counseling staff or someone in your church who can act as an advocate (a sponsor in AA language) while the addict is receiving counseling. I've never done drugs myself, so I don't know how it feels. But, I do know that these drugs are incredibly powerful and that God is needed to get them out of it. Make no mistake about it, the life of the addict is a horrible life. Have a little compassion here or someday it may be you in need of a little compassion (Prov. 16:18).

How this can help your ministry

First, let's talk about how not to help. Let's not be harsh. Remember Galations 6:1, did you also notice a "spirit of gentleness" in the passage? I hope so because what so often happens in these cases is that the user's self-centered sins creep over into the lives of the people around them. This can create anger, which is also self-centered. Ugh! People, we must be careful how we talk to them. Be gentle and kind.

Second, Ephesians 4:29 says, "Let no unwholesome word proceed from your mouth, but only such *a word* as is good for edification according to the need *of the moment*, so that it will give grace to those who hear." This is true for all of us but especially with addicts. Constant criticism or condescension will drive them to cover up even more. But words, that are edifying, gracious and timely, will have a greater longer-term effect than we know. Folks, this is a command from God here. We do not have the option to be harsh any more than they have the option to do drugs. So, again, I say, be gentle and kind.

Third, don't take it personally. When a loved one lies to you, it can feel as though they no longer love or respect you, and this can cause a great amount of emotional pain. I get it. I've been to this movie and boy does it hurt. You must remember, that although an addict mainly lies for their own benefit – to keep the reality of their situation from surfacing, they also lie because they believe that by lying to a loved one, it is causing them less pain with a 'what you don't know won't hurt you' type of attitude. Instead of getting upset and yelling at them or reacting negatively towards them, take it with a grain of salt and focus your energy on helping them get out of their situation instead.

Fourth, don't enable. Stop covering up for them. Allow them to suffer the consequences for their sin. And, stop acting as if you don't know when you do know. If you know that your loved one is lying to you, pretending to believe them, or turning a blind eye will encourage their behavior, sinking them deeper into their addiction. Whether they think you actually believe them, or they know you're turning a blind eye, you're essentially telling them that their behavior is okay. Instead, you need to let them know that you know the truth. When the lies are no longer working, it will help force them into honesty and (hopefully) into asking for the help they need.

Fifth, as with many counselees, provide information that might influence the addict to make up their own minds to change instead of you trying to persuade them to change. They have to make the decision on their own. Help them see the two paths they're on and then let them make their own choice. Deuteronomy 30:15 puts it this way, "See, I have set before you today life and prosperity, and death and adversity." One path leads to death. The other leads to life. You can't stop an addict from being an addict, but you can help them see the choice and ramifications of their choices. That is what God did for us. We can do that for him.

Sixth, trust your instincts. Because addicts become amazingly skilled at lying, you are not required to believe his lies. If a person's behavior changes markedly and the explanations don't really add up, you have to hold to your common sense. If what you're being told doesn't make sense, it doesn't add up, then there's probably a very good reason—you're being lied to. Trust your instincts.

Last, you can ask an addict to tell you the truth but don't expect him to give it to you. In fact, expect him to lie. This is what happened with my addict buddy.

I was so frustrated with a string of previous counselees lying right to my face that I sat down with this young man and asked him if he was using again. I told him right up front, "If I find out you are lying, I will never speak to you again. We will be done. I mean done, done. Done!" With that, I asked him if he had ever used meth and he said, no. I put on a face of belief but in my head, because of some other information I had, I was pretty sure he was lying. Still, I had hoped he wasn't, but as it turns out, he was. So, now what was I to do?

Being the sucker I am, I took him back in. I told him what he needed to do and that I would not lift a finger to help him. He would have to do it all by himself. And, he did. He got himself into an outpatient help program. After six months, we started counseling and his life and marriage got put back together.

I tell you that story to illustrate that it was unhelpful and unnecessary for me to ask my addict counselee to tell me the truth when I knew he was going to lie. Folks, all addicts are liars until they are no longer addicts. Even then, their lying, being so ingrained, may take years to get rid of. So whether you ask them to tell you the truth or not, don't expect it.

Lessons Learned

Chapter 16

What's the rush?

(Psalm 27)

Suppose for a minute, a couple comes to you for some dating advice. They are both in the final stages of a divorce. Consider first that the divorce is a fait accompli, a done deal as we say in the USA. It's not a matter of if; it's a matter of when. They've been waiting 2 years for the courts to finalize the paperwork. These two people love each other and as soon as their divorces are final, they plan on tying the knot. They come to you because they are not sure it's ok for them to be dating yet and they want to know if they should stop what they're doing and wait for the courts to get it done. What will you tell them?

Meet Ed and Roberta

Ed and Roberta go to a super solid bible-believing church. Roberta is new in the Lord, Ed being more mature in his faith. In fact, he's in the ministry as a lay-person. Roberta is coming out of a bad marriage. She was abused by an unfaithful husband. Double ouch. Ed was married to a woman who ended up on drugs. In fact, they both were until Ed got saved. His wife did not get saved and ended up committing adultery. Due to unfaithful, sexually immoral acts on the part of both Ed's wife and Roberta's husband, each had the biblical out to get divorced and took it.

Two year later, they're still married, waiting for their divorces to be final. Perhaps, the most interesting thing here is that even though they each had the "out," and all they were waiting on was the court system to do their job, they both wondered if they should be dating before the divorce was final. Well, they didn't wait. They dated and when their divorces were final, they got married. Fast forward 2 years, and they're in my office. Uh, oh!

Uh, oh, is right. This was back in the financial crisis in the early 2000s. Money was tight. They had several homes, mostly under water. Both of them worked like dogs just to be able to make ends meet. Their jobs and their home were stressful. Even church was stressful because they could not find one that they both enjoyed. They both had kids coming into the marriage and then had one of their own. Yikes, right?! You can see that they had a lot of "life" working against them, but they still had their faith and that should have helped them.

Ed was mature in his knowledge of the Bible, but he proved himself to be domineering and controlling. He was often angry at her, the kids, his boss, his employees, and probably me at some point. His anger resulted in raised voices and crazy accusations. I liked this guy but man, this dude was intense, and Roberta, coming from an abusive relationship, hurt easy and would have a hard time letting it go.

Roberta was young in her faith. Most of what I taught them was new to her and she was very willing to try. The problem was that it was never good enough for Ed. The communication was bad, and understandably, sex was irrelevant to her. Roberta, immature in her faith, lived in fear, trying to please Ed. What she would hear from him is that this is all your fault and sadly, she actually believed it. That's not exactly a turn-on for a woman.

Within the first 2 weeks of counseling, they confessed that they shouldn't have dated before her divorce was final. Each wondered, "if we hadn't dated, maybe we wouldn't be stuck in a bad marriage again.

The principle

Back to my original question, "if they had come to you while they were dating, what would you have told them?" Well, before you give a trite answer, let me play both sides of the issue. One side says it's simple, you shouldn't date because you are married. You are not divorced. You are married. Why is this a complicated question?! Of course you shouldn't date! You need to leave room for God to work in your spouse's heart until the divorce is final. Then you can think about marriage.

The other side says the only hang up here is today's government in this country. In other parts of the world, you'd be done in a day. In biblical times, you just had to write it on a piece of paper and that was that. Under that reasoning, from the time you file for a divorce, you are now divorced so you can date.

So, which is it? What do you think? Is the Bible clear on this or is it grey? So, there they are in your office asking you, the pastor, elder, counselor, mentor, friend. What's your opinion and why? So, here's mine: don't date until the divorce is final. You ask, why?

Well, first, I don't think it's trite to say you're married. You *are* married and can file taxes as a married couple, which is a huge advantage.

Second, in our country, you are not married until the government says you are nor are you divorced until it says you are. You got married under those rules. Abide by them.

Third, and this is the kicker, I have had 5 couples in my office stuck in bad marriages who had began dating before their divorces were final. Some knew they shouldn't. Some didn't. Some got advice from a pastor to wait and didn't. Some got no advice at all and just did what they wanted. In all 5 cases, they all thought in the back of their mind that, "hey, if we would have just waited until the divorce was final, maybe we would not have dated, and maybe we would not have gotten married."

How this can help your ministry

One of the goals of this book was to let my years of experience teach you something or illustrate to you something that may not be as black in white in the Scriptures as we'd like. Don't murder. Don't steal. Don't covet. Those are easy. The question in this chapter is maybe not so clear. At least some people think that way. For me, I think the Scripture is clear and I believe my personal experience bears that out.

As a biblical counselor, I am a believer in the total absolute sufficiency of Scripture. In it, we have everything we need for life and godliness. Romans 13 clearly states that we are to obey our government unless it is asking you to sin against God. As individuals, we do not get to say when one is married or divorced. Currently, our government is the one that pronounces marriage and divorce. Someday soon, this may no longer be the case, but for today, it is what it is. So, for me, it's clear. You are married until you are divorced, and no married people should be dating anyone other than their spouse.

On the practical side, I hope it is also abundantly clear. Five couples came to me this way. I am sure there are couples out there who married early and their marriages are fine, but I've had 5 who had the opposite experience. Should we ignore their stories?

Listen, if God wants you to be married, you'll be married. Don't force the issue. Wait for God to work through the governments that He is in control of. We are such impatient people by nature. It just seems to me that it's a good idea to learn some patience before you're married so that you can exercise it better after you're married.

Keeping it real simple, what's the rush, people? You really can't wait one or two more months? Save yourself some serious trouble and learn from those who've been in my office, stuck in a bad marriage, and wait. Counselors, pastors, elders, tell your people to wait on goodness of the Lord (Ps. 27).

Lessons Learned

Section 2

Messages of Hope

Steve Mawhorter

Lessons Learned

Chapter 17

Can your marriage survive an affair?

(Psalms 42)

Yes, and even the victims of the affair can come to Christ during the incident. These two stories will challenge the perception that affairs cannot be overcome.

According to the APA, 50% of men and women cheat on their spouses, but only 20-40% of those marriages end in divorce. Another study noted that 75% of marriages survived the affair if it was the man who committed adultery whereas only 65% of marriages survive if it's the woman who had the affair. Either way, about 70% of marriages survive. It's nice to have some stats behind us, isn't it. Actual success stories help as well. Here's one.

Meet Heather and Doug

Doug and Heather go to a solid church. Heather is a believer. Doug is not, but he attends faithfully. They have children and are doing a good job raising them. Money is not an issue for them. On the outside, all looks well. However, it was not so on the inside.

Inside the home, Doug was cold, distant, and not much of a talker. He was into his job, not his marriage. Though he faithfully attended church, he just didn't believe. Still, he would try and lead his family as was taught in the church.

Heather, on the other hand, was a firecracker. She was emotional, lively, energetic, and a real talker. She craved friendships. She craved love from Doug but just didn't get it from him. As he tried to lead, she dug her heels in and fought him on almost every front.

They were in a bad pattern—prideful and arrogant, which is at the heart of adultery. Heather didn't feel loved and Doug didn't feel respected. You can see where this one's heading, can't you? Well, you're right, but I'll bet not as right as you thought.

I bet that you thought that Doug, the unbeliever, would step out on Heather, that he'd find someone who respected him and enjoyed his personality. Well, that is not what happened. It was Heather, the believer, who was vulnerable here. Remember, she craved love. She met someone within the flow of everyday life and they began to share their thoughts. Soon, those thoughts became intimate thoughts, physical touch being inevitable. So, it happened. They started an affair.

Doug sniffed it out as most men do. It is only the most clever and conniving of the females that can keep it from their husbands and she wasn't that clever. Doug confronted her one day and she did what most people do. They lie. In her mind, she had to lie. If she didn't, she'd be divorced with several kids and not enough money to survive, so of course she lied. Doug chose to believe her on the outside, but on the inside, he knew she was having an affair. The story gets even more interesting here.

While Heather was having her affair, the Holy Spirit began working on Doug, the unbeliever. He'd been attending church with Heather for years and years and though he liked what he heard, it all went in one ear and out the other. It just never landed for him. Then, just when you would think he'd bag the marriage and Christianity in total, the Spirit got a hold of him. God opened his unbelieving eyes and made a new man out of him. Heather could see it, but she was stuck in her affair. She'd already moved on, so she thought.

Well, a few months passed, and soon the Holy Spirit went to work on Heather, too. She was overwhelmed with guilt and shame. She couldn't take it anymore, so she did what most Christians do, and she ended the affair and confessed to Doug what she had done. She asked for forgiveness and to start over. They came to me and we started over together.

It was early that spring that Doug contacted me and told me the story. I then met with Heather and heard her side. I then got the two of them in the same room. It wasn't pleasant. He was angry, bitter, and hard. She was ready for a do-over. She expected he'd be excited and prepared to move on. She couldn't understand why he couldn't just forgive and move on. By the way, as stated in a previous chapter, all perps are this way. They're always ready to move on and impatient that others can't forgive them as fast as they ended the affair. If you're one whose spouse forgave quickly, count your blessings.

As you might expect, Doug and Heather's relationship suffered because of many problems that had built up over time. Our sessions were long and lasted for many months (Rome wasn't built in a day). She had to see her disrespect and she did. He had to see that her vulnerability came due to his lack of love for her, and he did. And, most of all, praise the Lord that during the six months I saw them, their relationship improved a great deal and praise Him even more because their marriage is healthy and their relationship has improved. It is great to see what God can do.

The principles

So, how does a marriage survive an affair? There are several key components. First, there needs to be an open and honest confession and all contact between the adulterers must end. The adulterers do not need a closure conversation. That will end in the furtherance of the affair. They need to get out of Dodge asap and end all contact where possible (Prov. 5:8; 1 Cor. 10:14).

Two, there needs to be a full recommitment by both parties, husband and wife, to God and each other. This is not, "well, let's give it a try and see how it works out." That attitude is a bad seed and it will not work out. One or the other will get out before they can work it out.

Three, attitudes must change. Each must see their pride, arrogance, and selfishness. They cannot focus on their spouse's issues. Let the pastor/counselor do that. Matt. 7:5 says, "First, get the board out of your own eye . . . " And, speaking of the pastor/counselor, that's number four on my list. Don't try this one alone. Get some help.

Four, they need to figure out how they got to the place where they are. It doesn't matter who had the affair. It could easily have been Doug in this case. He was just as vulnerable. He just wasn't as available as Heather. What was wrong in the marriage that got them here? The pastor can help them with that.

Five, and there could be many more than this, but this one is the most important. It is a recommitment to one's faith. God first, others second, me, last. In fact, in my opinion, I'm not even on the list of importance. God will take care of me. I'm not on that list. Everyone else is, but not me. So, what do I mean by God first?

I mean worship. In Revelation (Rev. 5:8-10, when the elders see Jesus, they fall on their faces and sing a song. When sin has been revealed like this, both people are going to Jesus in a different way. Both should get on their knees together, bow their heads, and pray. Both should get to church, sing songs like they've never sung before. And, by the way, if this ever happens to you, don't be surprised if you can't finish some songs without tears running down your face.

You'll feel shame like you never have before. You'll know grace as you've never known it. You'll experience mercy you've never seen before. There's a song we sing now called **His Mercy is More**.

The lyrics go like this:

Praise the Lord!
His mercy is more
Stronger than darkness, new every morn
Our sins, they are many, His mercy is more

Yes, you'll know mercy as you've never known it, and this song will bring tears down your face. You'll think, "everyone's looking at me," but listen, we're all thinking that. We are all sinners in need of the mercies of God and we have a great God who loves to give it.

How this can help your ministry

These are just a few of the steps needed to make the marriage last, but listen, please listen. These marriages can be better than ever and likely will. Will it be perfect? No. No one has a perfect marriage, not even mine, though it's pretty fantastic. It's not perfect because we are not perfect people. Neither of us gets everything we want. We are not immune to the imperfections and discontent of the other.

Nonetheless, these marriages can be so much more than they've ever experienced. Teach them to be thankful for whatever God graces them with. Encourage them to raise their kids and keep those skeletons in the closet. Encourage them to thank their pastor for his love and commitment to them and to tell him how much they appreciate him.

Lessons Learned

Last, remind them that God is good all the time, and, all the time, God is good. And, because He is good, there is always hope if their hope is in God, so don't let them give up hope (Ps. 42). Their marriage truly can be better than ever.

Steve Mawhorter

Lessons Learned

Chapter 18

You never know

(Acts 8-10; 1 Cor. 5:11)

Meet Ben and Emma

Of all the stories I tell, this is one of my very favorites, if not my most favorite. Put your seat belt on for this one.

In the latter years of their life, Ben and Emma came to us because they were having marriage problems. During my initial interview with them, they shared their testimony with me. It's one for the record books and I would like to share that with you in this chapter so that you will never say never again.

Ben was a pimp. How's that for a beginning! Yes, he was a pimp and a large one to boot. He was in organized crime. His entire life was engulfed by evil. There were pushers and users, pimps and prostitutes, robbers and killers. He himself was drunk, a doper, a whore monger, a pornographer, a thief, and a fence for stolen securities. He lived a gutter life, a lifestyle of death. He was totally engrossed in his own sin, even more than what I've even already written here.

Then, we have Emma, his wife. Yes, hard to believe it, but this man was married. She was sweet and feisty, needy and moody, impressionable, trusting, angry, bitter, and hopeless. Emma was also a prostitute, his prostitute. Yep, you got it. He had convinced her to be a prostitute for him. There is no point in explaining how this was logical. It wasn't. To him, it was, but she knew in her heart, though she was not a believer, obviously, she knew this was wrong. The truth is written on our hearts, right? And, it was written on hers. She knew it was wrong but out of fear, she obeyed her husband.

Ben and Emma were unbelievers, blind to sin. They knew they had to get out of organized crime. They knew they were on a death march, but to get out and not be killed, they would have to leave the state and that they did. They packed up and moved thousands of miles away and restarted life.

When they arrived in their new State, they needed jobs. With no experience and no education, Ben and Emma became taxi drivers. It was a far cry from what they were doing before and though it didn't pay much, it paid enough for them to back on their feet and feed their children. Yeah, children! Crazy, huh?

While they were there, they met another driver who loved to give out Christian tracts to people. One day, he gave one to Ben and Emma. After reading the tract, Ben and Emma became believers, right there on the spot. They now have several children, all of whom went on to Christian school. One even became a counselor, a biblical counselor.

Fast forward twenty years and they are in my office having marriage troubles. As is often the case, the bottom line was that he was not feeling respected and she didn't feel loved. Truth is, he was not respected in his home and he was not loving his wife. As a result, they were having trouble communicating with each other.

The world's counsel would be to spend time going over and over the past, but our take was to stick to the present problems at hand. God had forgiven the past and it had nothing to do with the present, so we spent time talking about the purpose of marriage, the roles of the husband and wife, anger and forgiveness, and of course, communication and conflict resolution.

During our time with them, they realized that pride, apathy, sarcasm, and debt, had crept into their marriage, making problems seem insurmountable. Over time, they learned to make better decisions together. He learned how lazy he was and how to love his wife a little better, though not perfectly. She learned the importance of listening and the value of biting her tongue. Both learned the value of being a grace-giver.

All in all, they were good people, enjoyable people. The passage that comes to mind with Ben and Emma is found in 1 Cor. 5:11, "Or do you not know that the unrighteous will not inherit the kingdom of God? Do not be deceived; neither fornicators, nor idolaters, nor adulterers, nor effeminate, nor homosexuals,[10] nor thieves, nor *the* covetous, nor drunkards, nor revilers, nor swindlers, will inherit the kingdom of God. ¹¹ Such were some of you; but you were washed, but you were sanctified, but you were justified in the name of the Lord Jesus Christ and in the Spirit of our God." They were all of that, key word being *were*. They were not that any longer. God had miraculously changed them so that by the time they came to us, they were very moldable and easy people to work with.

The principle

You never know. God can save anyone at any time in any way He chooses. No one is out of reach. No one has gone too far to be saved. Who would have believed that two people, a pimp and his whore, immersed in organized crime, could escape and find Christ? The truth for most of us is that if we were the taxi driver that gave them the tract, and we had known who they were, we would have kept the tract and given it to someone else that looked more likely to be savable. Most of us are looking for the low-hanging fruit. Ben and Emma would not have looked like low-hanging fruit to anyone, but neither would have the apostle Paul. God forgive us for our unbelieving spirits.

How this can help your ministry

Every person who comes to your office is reachable. You should never look at anyone and think, *"no way."* God saved Cornelius, the Ethiopian Treasurer in Acts 8, Paul in Acts 9, the Roman solider in Acts 10. Why could he not save a pimp and his whore? Why can he not save those right there in front of you? Just get you and your doubts out of the way and give them the gospel. God brought them to you. They are not there by accident. Your meetings with unbelievers are not accidents, people. They are divine appointments. I had one such divine appointment several years ago.

This young couple came into my office, knowing no one at our church. They knew nothing about God and the wife had never even heard of the Bible. Yes, never even heard of it. They came because they were having marriage issues. After hearing their non-testimony, I dropped all my plans to talk about marriage, and shared the gospel with them. We talked about the Bible and how God wants us to live. Our conversation was only an hour, but it was life-changing for them. The following week, they prayed to receive Christ.

You see, every person who dawns the door of your church has been brought there by the sovereign, providential hand of an all-loving, all-wise, all-powerful, faithful, gracious, and merciful God. Romans 10:17 says, "So faith *comes* from hearing, and hearing by the word of Christ." How will they come if someone will not preach to them the gospel and how will you preach the gospel if you do not believe someone is savable? They are all savable. You never know. Never say never. Preach it, brother!

Lessons Learned

Chapter 19

Women are not complicated

(Eph. 5:25, 28)

Meet Howard and Heather

Howard and Heather are a young married couple with several kids. Both are believers. Heather grew up in a solid, super conservative family. She greatly desired purity in her life before and after marriage. Before they were married, he respected the physical boundaries she wanted, but still pushed her a little further than she wanted to go. That proved to be a seed of trouble for them in the future.

A couple of years after they were married, Howard began using pornography. Pornography use has reached epidemic levels not only in the United States, but worldwide. Where there is a computer and the internet, porn is instantly there at the click of a button. It is an ugly beast and a tool of Satan that he expertly uses to try and break up couples and destroy lives.

As is often the case in Christian marriages, the Lord's heavy hand of conviction moved Howard to confess his sin to Heather. Praise God, she forgave him, and Howard immediately joined an accountability group for other men who struggled with porn. Though I'm not a huge fan of groups like these where, typically, the blind lead the blind, it was helpful for Howard. He distanced himself from pornography, going about eight months without it, and Heather seemed to be healing from the hurt and betrayal of trust caused by his porn use.

Sadly, he began dabbling in porn again. Two years later, the beast of addiction had returned in full force. Once again, God moved Howard to confess his sin to Heather and rejoin the accountability group. She forgave him again, and they started anew—until he started watching porn a third time. Unfortunately, the third time was not the charm. This time his confession was not met with mercy. Not only could Heather not forgive Howard, but she wanted out of the marriage. That's when Howard came to me for counseling. Deeply wounded and angry, Heather refused to attend.

Howard and I met many times over the next several months. While his heart was broken, Heather's was hardening. He didn't know what to do. I explained that while his sexual sin was an issue, the bigger problem was that he was not loving his wife sacrificially and unconditionally as commanded by Ephesians 5:25: "Husbands, love your wives, just as Christ also loved the church and gave Himself up for her."

Howard consistently described Heather as a pure woman who loved the Lord, which gave me a lot of hope. My experience is that women like that do not leave their marriages if their husbands love them like Christ loves the Church. "Until you do that," I told him, "evidenced by giving yourself to her and never engaging again with porn, her heart will remain hard. You need to be steadfast and immovable in your love for her, and trust God that He will not let her go."

It wasn't easy for Howard. Heather left their home as soon as he arrived from work each day and did not return until midnight. Occasionally, and with caution, Howard asked his wife where she went and what she was doing. She told him she was either sitting at a coffee shop or in her car, but he was concerned she had perhaps started up a relationship with another man who was encouraging her to divorce him. His belief in her purity was being sorely tested by her actions.

I reached out to her a couple of times through email to see if she would meet with me. I wanted to hear her side of the story and to see if I could encourage her in some way. She refused me as well. All she ever told me (in an email) was that she was done with the marriage and wanted out. She was wounded, and she didn't believe his confession nor accept his repentance. Yet she still came home each night and never filed for divorce. Why? To this day, I don't know—but the fact that she did not file, that gave me hope Howard and Heather could work things out.

I had listened to him describe his wife to me. In short, his descriptions were of a pure woman who loved the Lord. With that, I believed that she would return to the marriage if he would just keep loving her. You see, women do not leave their husbands who love them like Christ loves the church. He had never truly done that, but he was doing that now and needed to be steadfast and immovable in his love for her and trust God that He would not let her go.

Well, it took months and months, but she did return. It takes time for ice to melt and Rome wasn't built in a day, right? Her heart was hard, but her heart was still with the Lord, and in the end, it was God's love and her husband's love that put this humpty dumpty marriage back together again. All glory goes to the Lord.

The principle

Women are not complicated. They just want to be truly and fully loved. I'll always remember my three years of coaching girls basketball for our local Christian high school after coaching the boys squad for the previous 18 years.

I discovered that for the boys, it's all about the win. How we got there was not important. For the girls, though, it was more about the journey than the win. Yes, they focused on how they're going to wear their hair, or what they're doing after the game, or who's going to homecoming. But far more than that, the girls I coached wanted to feel loved by the men in their lives, whether that was their boyfriend, dad, or me as their coach. If they felt loved by me, they would've run through a wall for me. (Well, only after looking at me like I was some kind of weirdo.)

Then came the day that I said something that hurt one of the girl's feelings. She didn't give me a dirty look or say anything in response, but I could see in her face that what I said, or the way I said it, had hurt her. I knew right away that I needed to talk to her when practice was over. Before she left, I apologized and told her that I really appreciated her and cared a great deal for her. Even though I could tell she was still wounded, her countenance changed. The next day, she was all smiles, and we ended up bonding closer than before. A genuine expression of love, and the healing balm of time, made all the difference.

Is it any wonder, then, that *the* command God gave husbands was to love their wives as Christ loves us? Women want to know they are loved by the men in their lives, and they need to be given the time for their wounds to heal. It doesn't matter, guys, if you meant to hurt them or not. You can't just command their feelings to go away. Love is patient, right? Be patient and earn back their trust in you.

How this can help your ministry

The world tells us all the time that women are complicated and they make jokes about it. I've heard it in Christian circles, too. "Live with your wives in an understanding way. How are we supposed to do that? Who can understand 'em." "Women are impossible, right? Wrong. Different? Yes. Tell those husbands the truth. Women are not complicated.

Are women more emotional? Probably so, but that does not make them more impossible or complicated than men. Do they have PMS problems that men don't have? Probably so, but we have our own issues and our issues are not physical in nature. Are they hard to figure out? No, they are easy. All your wife wants is to feel loved. If she feels loved, you'll know it. If she does not, you'll know that, too.

When a couple comes to you for help, there will almost always be two people who both have changes to make. Start with the husband. If he is truly loving his wife like Christ loves the church, in due time, you'll see changes in her. If, in those rare occurrences, months go by and you still don't see any changes in her, you can now address her bitterness and doubts with a little more fervor.

From my life experience, I have met many men who have left their wives even though they respected their husbands, but I have yet to find a woman who has left a man who loved her like Christ loves the church. Men, if she's being difficult, and if you have the guts, ask her on a scale of 1-10, how loved she feels by you. I'll just bet you that you'll get her attention and learn something about yourself. You start loving her more and you just watch her change (Eph. 5:28). That's what happened with Howard and Heather. It can happen to you, too.

Gentlemen, prove me wrong on this one. I dare you!

Lessons Learned

Chapter 20

I don't think I can take anymore!

(1 Cor. 10:13)

Meet Harry and Wanda

Harry and Wanda are in their 20s and have been married for less than 2 years. Both claim to be solid believers; in fact, both help out with worship at the church, Bob for at least 5 years. Neither of them however, read their Bibles. This is where the similarities end.

Harry came from a solid Christian home. He's a pretty serious guy and a bit on the shy side. Wanda is just the opposite. She comes from a broken home, is not shy at all and though she can be serious, she is much more prone to laughter than Harry. While Harry grew up in a good Christian home, Wanda's parents were drug addicts and physically abusive. Wanda was sexually molested at 7 and later in her very early teens. She was taken by Child Protective Services on 2 separate occasions. Her parents divorced when she was 14, which she says is when all her problems began. Think about that for a second. She'd been sexually molested twice before she was 15, yet it wasn't until her parents' divorce that all her problems began.

Soon after they married, Harry lost his job and Wanda developed a friendship with a girl, something she had never had before, a "bff." Wanda swears they are just friends, but Harry suspects something more is going on between the two of them. By the time they got to me, they were already distant from each other, sitting on opposite couches and not talking at all.

In our first meeting, I learned that Harry's response to what he thought might be a homosexual affair was to get jealous, angry, talk to his parents, and become distant from Wanda, burying his head in the TV, even looking at pornography a few times. He has a new job now that only requires him to work 9 to 5 and his commute is short. The job pays well enough to pay their bills but due to her schooling, they have racked up a lot of school debt. The good news there is that when she does get her job, and she will, they will have those paid off in 2 years. Hey, a ray of sunshine, we all thought together.

Wanda revealed that she'd been anorexic during their first year, losing 27 lbs. She also revealed that she'd been cutting herself, though not too often. Cutting often goes along with anorexia so that wasn't too surprising. Wanda is on medication for depression, anxiety, migraines, and birth control. Further, Wanda says that she has pretty severe sleep problems perhaps due to stress, migraines, anxiety, depression and has had some suicidal thoughts, though not serious, just "I'd rather be dead than live like this" thoughts. Due to her schooling background, she is pretty psychologized in her way of thinking. She tells me that the only real positive thing in her life right now is her new *bff*, something she has never had before. You're thinking, "oh boy, I can see where this is going."

When they finally got to me, they presented me with this: Harry felt neglected and Wanda felt controlled. They indicated that they just needed help communicating so that they could understand each other better. Sound overwhelming? Well, this was just the tip of the iceberg!

Over the next 5 months, we would meet another 10 times. I found both of them to be very humble and teachable, so following 2 Timothy 3:16-17, "All Scripture is inspired by God and profitable for teaching, for reproof, for correction, for training in righteousness; so that the man of God may be adequate, equipped for every good work," I began with simple instructions on marriage and gave them a few new house rules, which they followed.

While watching TV "together" on separate couches, Wanda would text her *bff*. Guys love that, you know. We love it when we are with our wives while they are texting with someone else. You know I'm kidding, right?

The fact is, she could have been texting with Jesus, and Harry would have felt slighted. I'm sure that in Harry's mind, he thought, "well if that's who you'd rather be with, then just go be with her!" Good thing he didn't say that because it was true at the time. So, because love gives preference and love is never rude, instruction one for her was no texting your *bff* when you are with your husband.

Instruction one for Harry was super simple, NO MORE TV. All men, everywhere should hear that instruction! Turn it off boys. Grow up. Take an interest in your wife. Maybe if you weren't watching TV, she wouldn't be on her phone with her *bff.*

Instruction two was for them: no more yelling. It always blows me away how much two Christian people who say they love each other will still yell at each other. Listen, people. I have never raised my voice at my wife one time, not once! I may have wanted to, but I never have. I tell all my counselees, "no more yelling this week. You're done doing that." They look at me with their eyes crossed as if that's an impossible task. I give them some duct tape. That usually adds a little humor and helps make the point.

Instruction three was to get back into their bibles and to start praying together. All couples think they have no time for this but when you take their pacifiers away (a.k.a. TV and internet), it's amazing how much free time they have to read anything I give them.

Instruction four was to memorize 2 Cor. 5:9, "Therefore we also have as our ambition, whether at home or absent, to be pleasing to Him." I wanted them to start thinking, moment by moment, what would be pleasing to God?

During this time, I gave them two videos to watch on the roles of marriage. These are videos of a class that I have taught for over 20 years. They got to see my mug a lot during these many months. I also assigned them two books to read, *The Exemplary Husband* by Stuart Scott for him and *Helper By Design* by Elyse Fitzpatrick for her.

These were all different patterns of living that I was trying to ingrain into their daily lives: Turn your attention away from other forms of entertainment and turn towards each other. Stop being rude. Read your bible and pray. Read another book that explains the bible, in this case books that explain what the Bible says about marriage. We were off to a good start, so I thought.

Well, pretty quickly, the house rules went out the door and in came the flesh. They stopped reading, went back to their vices, and came in pretty discouraged. I decided we need to start over.

After hearing their full testimonies again, and realizing that Harry could not find the book of James, I decided that I had given them too much credit for their understanding of scriptural things, so we went back to the basics. They needed to learn more about God than marriage so I assigned them a sermon to listen to that I had done on the providence of God from Ps. 46:10,

"Be still and know that I am God." And I had asked them to read a chapter out of *Systematic Theology* by Wayne Grudem on the same topic.

These were foundational pieces to their growth and the pace of counseling began to pick up. They were doing really well until God began to give Wanda what Wanda didn't want and take what she didn't want Him to take. To be honest, what God gave and took, was even a little bit much for me. Listen to what God would throw at her during our next several months of counseling.

Wanda's sister would move away, taking with her Wanda's nephew, who Wanda treated as if it was her own. Wanda will lose her first and only *bff*. Harry, by the way, wasn't rejoicing over this. He had realized this was really Wanda's first and only real friend and there was nothing sinister about it. He was very compassionate towards her. Well, if that wasn't enough, Wanda would get a rare disease that would cause her to miss school and work for a week. This is a lot for anyone to go through and I distinctly remember one session where Wanda came in crying hysterically that she just couldn't take anymore. Well, she was wrong.

Soon after this, the church they'd been involved with since it started, folded due to a moral failure by the pastor. And, to top it all off, God would take her father. That was the kicker for me. I thought, "come on God! Really!" We had been making some real progress with her and her husband was being very loving and maturing spiritually. "Why now?!"

Wondering how all this turned out?

They needed to get two main things straight. First, they were each totally self-focused. Aren't we all? Yes, but at least those that are more mature know this about themselves. These two were clueless. Second, they needed to know God better, particularly His providence. Thankfully, learning both of these made each of them so much stronger by the time we finished.

Wanda was eating regularly and not cutting. She was no longer depressed and had learned to be open and vulnerable with Harry like she used to be with her *bff*. She no longer saw sex as an obligation and was now enjoying it. Harry had learned that he was deathly afraid of his wife's approval, something very common in men, and this had been the driving force in his life. By the time we had finished, she had read *Depression A Stubborn Darkness, Love to Eat Hate to Eat, Helper By Design,* and part of *Systematic*

Theology by Wayne Grudem. Harry finished *The Exemplary Husband* and together, they read pamphets by Jay Adams on marriage but most importantly, Harry was reading his bible again.

The principle

"I don't think I can take anymore!" I hate it when I hear that. Often times, when I hear that, knowing that they *can* take more, I know that God is going to give them more. And, with this couple he did. Out of nowhere, just when they were doing really well, God took Wanda's Dad. You would think that would have devastated her, but you know what, it didn't. Both she and Harry had grown so much that they found they could take more and handle it well. And, they did. But, how is that possible?

Well, by the time we were finished, they got it. They totally understood that all of their problems were due to their own self-focus in life. They learned about idols of the heart, those longings inside that drive us to think what we think, feel what we feel, and do what we do. And, because they came to understand the providence of God, their fears were gone. They believed in God. They just didn't know him beyond the level of an acquaintance. They were so much more mature when they left. I miss them.

How this can help your ministry

There are several lessons in this. One, don't be afraid to tell a hurting person the truth that the reason they are suffering to the level they are is not the circumstance. It's their own self-focus and lack of knowing and therefore trusting God. Tell people the truth in a loving way. Not every hard thing in life must be met with a puddle of tears for weeks and months. Think it through. When I told Wanda this, it hit her hard but the next week, she came back and said, "I guess what you're saying is that all my struggles are because I'm selfish. Is that correct?" With a smile of love and affection, I said, "yes. That is true." She said, "you're right. I am selfish." Tell them the truth in a loving way

Second, as a biblical counselor, you need to know the providence of God like the back of your hand. There are lots of resources out there, some already mentioned in this chapter, but to throw in one more, I suggest you read *Trusting God* by Jerry Bridges.

Three, never let your friends/counselees think they can't take anymore. That's a lie. They can take a lot more. I remember growing up that my Uncle would get me in a headlock and rub his knuckles on my head until I cried, *Uncle!* Never say you can't take anymore because God will likely give you more until you yourself cry uncle. It's better to cry it now. 1 Cor. 10:13 says, "No temptation has overtaken you but such as is common to man; and God is faithful, who will not allow you to be tempted beyond what you are able, but with the temptation will provide the way of escape also, so that you will be able to endure it." You can endure way more than you think when you know the One who saved you. Remember the words of Paul, "when I am weak . . . He is strong."

Lessons Learned

Chapter 21

Sauls into Pauls

(2 Cor. 5:17)

One thing I've learned is that God can do the most amazing things through the most unlikely people.

Meet Elaine

Elaine grew up in a bible believing church. She had invited Jesus into her heart when she was very, very young. She went to Christian school, vacation bible school, youth group and mission trips just like all the other *good* kids.

In the home, though Mom and Dad made it a point to protect Elaine from the outside world, they also invited that world into the home. They were weirdly legalistic about some grey area issues yet would bring other areas into the home that were obviously not grey. Due to the inconsistencies that Elaine saw in the home and her own curiosity about the big bad world, she began to show the signs of rebellion. Mom and Dad's bubble was about to burst.

While under their roof and right under their noses, Elaine started pursuing some extreme behaviors. She started sneaking out to party, drinking and smoking pot with her "friends." She got into some high-risk behaviors so much so that she would tell you that it's a wonder she didn't die. This went on for 2 years.

In her senior year, pondering her future, she thought she'd better change her life before it was too late. So, she tried to do the right things again. That meant going to church and even enrolling in a Christian college. Sounds good, right? Well, underneath the *good girl Christian who's coming back to the Lord*, was a desire to get away from her parents and do what her little heart wanted, and that was to party.

At her Christian school, she found more "friends" who would be just like her, professing/nominal, otherwise known as fake, Christians. All the old habits came back. Same stuff, just different people.

Then she met what she thought was a super godly guy, a guy with all the right theology except two little problems. One, why was a super godly guy interested in a not so super girl like Elaine? And, two, having sex before you were married was somehow not a problem for him. And since Elaine was into that anyway, it was a perfect fit. They got engaged and pursued premarital counseling. This is where the story turns. Their road to marriage was really her road to Damascus.

They ended up at a reformed church (remember his theology was right) and praise God, the counseling they received was from a church where biblical counseling was taught and lived out. Through the preaching and teaching, and the wise counsel from four ACBC certified counselors for a full year, their immoral lifestyle was exposed, and their relationship came to an end. He left the church. She got saved! My guess is the guy wouldn't give up the sex. Typical guy, eh?

During the next season of life, instead of smoking weed, Elaine would grow like one. The sermons were aimed right at her heart. For the first time, she understood that God loved her and that the Bible is truly His inspired Word. Without question, God had opened her eyes to believe. She read like she'd never read before and did homework. What a difference for her!

Elaine dove head-first into Wayne Grudem's *Systematic Theology*. She was given Dr. MacArthur's Study Bible and devoured it. And, like many others who have walked the same path she had, she became a fiery evangelist. But the story's not over.

A year later, she met the man who would become her husband. They received premarital counseling for 12 weeks, got married and moved from the bible belt to Babylon, otherwise known as Berkeley.

Their first year was difficult. Lots of fighting. Elaine says that, "had it not been for the premarital counseling they received, the marriage was doomed." But, because of the great counseling they received, they made it. So, where are they now?

Elaine, her husband, and their kids are at a solid bible teaching church with a biblical counseling program. They are on the premarital counseling team and have, at the time of this writing, counseled five couples into marriage. Elaine herself, is also one of the counselors at the church and is often given cases that are "right up her alley" if you know what I mean. Yeah, she is given those girls that are straying just like she did. She brings them what was brought to her, the truth in love.

The principle

I've learned that God can and will do the most amazing things through the most unlikely people. Think about it for a second. If you knew Elaine when she was in her darkness, would you imagine then where she is now?

If she came to your church with her testimony in hand, would you trust her with the hearts of your people or would you shy away from her thinking, "a leopard can't change its spots?" A lot of people think that, but is it true? NO, it is not true. In fact, God promises to change His people. We are new creatures with new desires. The old man is dead. The new man is alive and well (1 Cor. 6:11; 2 Cor. 5:17).

We have tons of people like Elaine here at NorthCreek Church who are counselors. We have former addicts, people who have been divorced, the sexually abused, people with debilitating diseases, newer believers, people who struggled with sexual sin, ex-gluttons, widows and widowers, cancer survivors, spouses with drug addicts for husbands, and so on. We even have people with psychology degrees who had to abandon all the gobbledygook that goes with it. Folks, we have some people who counsel who look like they belong, but we have a bunch more that, by the testimony of their former lives, most of you would not even take a second look at, and you would be wrong for thinking that way.

How this can help your ministry

Did not Saul turn into Paul? Was he not the most unlikeliest of men in the land to spread the gospel to the world? He himself describes himself as the chief of all sinners, worthy of death. Yet, was he not the best evangelist ever? Yes, he was.

As I write this, it occurs to me that there may be three audiences reading this chapter. You may be a church leader looking for counselors or you may be the person in the congregation who desires to help people like Elaine has. I have a word for both of you and another one for a potential third category.

For the church leader, there are no perfect people. There are only people. If they are true believers, and you see their faith already being lived out and they have a desire to help others, then train them. Your time is precious. Invest it into these people. They are going to help people who are going through issues that you have no experience in. Train them and turn them loose.

For those in the congregation who love God and want to help others out of trouble, come out of the shadows. Tell your story to your pastor. He will very likely receive you with open arms. If he doesn't, find a new church. Can I be any plainer than that? Find a new church. But, listen, it is most likely that your confession, your testimony, will be met with grace and mercy (Prov. 28:13). Talk to your pastor. Come up with a path for you to be trained and get busy helping people out of trouble.

There might be a third audience here. You might be one of those people who live in a town where the church you're at is the only one close to being biblical, yet they may receive your testimony with fear rather than love. You might be thinking that if you share your testimony and they reject you, then where will you go to church. That is a legitimate concern but not a legitimate fear.

Cast that fear aside. Go and talk to your pastor. If he rejects you, which again is highly unlikely, and if he is the only game in town, then get yourself trained online and help people in your church. In some cases, it might not be a bad idea for you to just start helping people under the radar for a while before you talk to the pastor, but that's your call.

Folks, my main point is like the title says, turn your Sauls into Pauls. Train them and turn them loose. Let others share in the same amazing grace that Elaine experienced. You won't be sorry.

Lessons Learned
Chapter 22

Guess who does our grief counseling?

(2 Cor. 1:3-7)

Meet Robert

Robert grew up with believing parents in what I would call a marginal, shallow church. He professed to be a believer in that church when he was 13 or 14 years old, but he would tell you now that he wasn't saved. Recently, he told me this, "nothing in my life reflected true faith or salvation, even though I had received Sunday school training in some of the bible."

After graduating college, Robert went off to college and avoided anything having to do with Christianity. It was in college that he met his first wife, also not a believer. They lived what would be called a 50/50 marriage or what we would call an egalitarian marriage, one where roles are shared equally. There is no head.

Well, though the way they chose to do marriage didn't work forever, they got along well enough to have children. After the children were born, using his upbringing, the Lord created a desire in Robert to have his kids trained at church where they would gain an understanding of the Christian faith. This would turn out to be a much greater blessing for him than he realized at the time.

Shortly after, the family (including his wife) joined a church where Robert was introduced to the doctrine of the *total depravity of man*. This was completely new to him, and even while he was still unsaved for years after that bible study, the concept kept grating on him. He kept asking himself, "am I really completely depraved?"

During that time, and still unsaved, the marriage was crumbling. She wasn't getting the affection and emotional support she wanted, and he wasn't getting what all men want, more sex. After 2 of their children went off to college, she asked Robert for a divorce. The Lord took Robert to his knees. It was during that time of sorrow that Robert acknowledgement his sin, and finally, at the age of 48, Robert got saved!

So now, Robert is a Christian, soon-to-be single, dad. What's next for him? Well, he got himself a new church and sat down with the pastor and told him his story. The pastor, Jon McNeff, charged Robert with going back to his soon-to-be ex-wife and doing everything he could to save his marriage. He did, but there was nothing he could do. Her mind was made up and they divorced. Now what?

The divorce hit him hard. He spent a year grieving and working through his bitterness towards his ex-wife. One night, in the summer of 2001, Robert woke up suddenly. He said he could feel the bitterness rising off of him. The Holy Spirit had changed his heart to be kind towards her, despite the divorce.

Robert took a year or so to grieve his divorce and then got back on the horse, so to speak. He went looking for a wife and found her at a local dance club, ballroom dancing that is, where he met Alice. Alice was a former Catholic and one who had searched many places for who God was. Robert and Alice really hit it off, but because she was an unbeliever, their relationship could go no further. So, he asked Alice if she would be willing to do a bible study with her on Wednesday nights and she agreed. Through that bible study, and after coming to an understanding that Jesus died a violent death on the cross to cover her sin, she made a profession of faith. Robert says, "I could see the lights go on in her eyes."

Though Robert took his time with Alice, they were married in June of 2004 about two years after they had initially met. That year, they enrolled in a class I've taught at NorthCreek Church for over twenty years now, called Cornerstone. It was a sweet time for them to bond but it was also during that time, only 6 months after they were married, that Alice developed breast cancer. Ugh!

After completing that class, and despite her cancer, they both believed that God had a purpose for them together as marriage counselors, so they started the first phase of counselor training in September of 2005. The second phase of our counseling training begins in May and goes through August. The week Alice started co-counseling in the summer of 2006 with another experienced NorthCreek Church counselor, Robert had to take her to the hospital. She was not doing well.

One month later, in August, Robert and Alice weren't at our weekly training session. Forty-five minutes into class, Robert came in, white as a ghost. I stopped class and asked, "Robert, are you ok?" He said, "I just found out Alice is going to die.

On September 21, 2006, Alice indeed passed away. He looks back now over their relationship and realizes that the Lord required her life that day, and he used him to help prepare her for Him. Though it was a short-lived relationship, he felt totally blessed to have had her, but he would again go through a time of grieving.

Yet undeterred, Robert decided he still wanted to be a counselor, something he would never have imagined years earlier when he was in his own words, "a self-centered, often angry, unrepentant sinner during that first marriage." So, again, it was time to get back on the horse and look for a wife. Can you guess what he did? Yep, he went back to the dance club, where he met who would be his third wife, Renee. They are now celebrating their ninth year of marriage and Robert still serves as one of our most treasured counselors.

Isn't it amazing what God does in people's hearts when they take the time to hear and understand His Word.

The principle

I learned that God can use anyone at any time and that he especially uses broken people to help other broken people (2 Cor. 1:3-7). I mean, who better to help someone who is in a hard marriage, or who is married to an unbeliever, or who is not yet even a Christian, or one who is newly divorced or a widower or married for the third time? How many guys are there out there who have been through all that Robert has been through?

How this can help your ministry

The natural thing is for us to look for those people who stand out publicly, who hold themselves together well. They talk and people listen. They talk the part and look the part. We tend to shy away from those who have been through some seriously hard knocks like Robert. Why do we do that?!

People who have been through hard times and are on the other side of those hard times, can really help others get through very difficult periods of life. They can say things to people that I can't say because I haven't been through anything like he has. He has permission just because! And, you know what, people will listen and do listen.

People like Robert, who have had many occasions to grieve, are gold. He started counseling with us shortly after Alice passed away in 2006. Look at some of the kinds of cases he has helped us with:

- Man with critical spirit toward his wife
- College kid who was addicted to video games and food
- 2 cases of adultery
- Husband left by a woman for her lesbian lover
- Man who was physically abused by his wife
- Habitual liar
- Homeless guy who hated white people
- Man married to an unfaithful wife

My encouragement to you is fourfold. First, find some broken people, fix them, and then turn them loose on others. Second, find people who have been through some seriously hard times and are now living victorious lives. If you think you don't have them in your church, tell your church that you are looking for them. I'll just bet you that they are sitting in your pews and you don't even know it. Ask them. Three, take your faithful attenders out to breakfast and ask them for their stories. You might be surprised at what you hear. You might have a Robert in your midst and you'll never know it unless you ask. Last, and not least, pray that God would deliver men like Robert to your church.

Lessons Learned

Chapter 23

Do people really get saved in counseling every year?

(Acts 9:18)

We receive phone calls nearly every month from pastors who have heard what we have been doing with biblical counseling in the bay area. They want to know what we do, how we do it, and if we can help them get something going like that in their church. We live for those moments.

Those *moments* usually take about two hours to have but they are worth it. Rarely do we have a meeting like that and yet that church doesn't follow through by starting something at their church. It may not be as formal as ours, but they get something started. Given that these are usually two-hour meetings, you can imagine that we pretty much exhaust most topics. That is true, but there is one common question that comes up that is worth a chapter in this book.

What they want to know is, "do people get saved through this ministry?" Happily, I can say absolutely. They get saved in many ways through this ministry. I'll give you one example.

Meet Peter and Mary

Now, before I get into this story, you have to remember a small detail about where we live. I referenced it in an earlier chapter of the book but have decided to rewrite that here. Take a look:

"My wife and I live in a home that faces 2 streets that both end in cul de sacs with a driveway that comes out on both streets, and we live behind a large high school. The students have found it a quicker getaway to drive up our street and through our driveway to come out the other side. Great for them. Not so great for us. Frequently during the year, students will actually do this. They ignore the fact that they are driving on our property to save only a couple of minutes."

Okay, hang on to that. Let's get back to Peter and Mary. They were a young married couple in their twenties. Peter's only background with Christianity was through Catholicism, but not because he was Catholic. He wasn't. There was no religious upbringing within his immediate family, but he was a difficult child. Not knowing what to do, his family placed him in a Catholic school during his eighth-grade year for one semester. They thought the Catholic school might keep him out of trouble.

When that semester ended, the family could not afford the tuition, so his little foray into religion ended. However, something did happen to him inside his soul. Though it was through the Catholic school, his experience there awakened in him the awareness of the existence of a god somewhere who was out there. He would say, *"that's when I first believed that God existed."* But, not finding the one true God there, he went back to his trouble-making life and didn't think much about it ever again.

Mary's story is similar and as sweet as my conversation with Peter was, it was even sweeter with Mary. I always ask for people's life story in counseling. I ask about family, school, important people and events. When I got to the question about school, it turned out that she went to the high school that sits immediately behind our house (see description above).

When she figured out which house was mine, I could see a little twinkle of guilt in her eyes. So I asked her, "So Mary, did you ever drive through my driveway?" She gasped and laughed and said "Yes, I'm so sorry." Well, we both laughed at that one and to be honest, Mary is not the only counselee I've had in my office that also drove through my driveway to save a little time. That little connection though made it easier to move into her religious upbringing.

When I asked Mary about that, she told me she had no religious upbringing whatsoever. When I say nothing, I mean nothing. Shocked, I asked her "Have you ever known anyone who was a Christian?" "Nope, was her answer." "Have you ever been to a church? "Nope." "Have you ever heard of the Bible?" "Nope." "So, you have never heard of the Bible at all?" "Nope."

This was a bit shocking for me. I was so flabbergasted that anyone could live in the United States and yet not have heard of the Bible. In my day, everyone would have heard of the Bible. As I gathered myself, I asked how they got to our church to come for counseling. They weren't actually sure. Someone, somewhere, had told Peter that he thought they did counseling at the church so they came. That was it. This was starting to feel like a God-moment.

I told them I was really glad they came and that it was obvious to me that God brought them here that day to meet me, the guy with the driveway Mary illegally drove through. I proceeded to share with them, very briefly, the gospel. I didn't ask them to pray a prayer. I didn't ask them if they believed what I was saying. I just told them the truth of the gospel.

Sadly, I also told them that my caseload was full but that I did have someone that I thought they would enjoy and could really help them. I gave them some homework that was centered around the gospel and I gave them bibles for them to use.

The counselor, Dan, was a short, sweet, 75-year-old man with lots of experience with younger people. Dan arranged their first meeting and I filled him in before they met. He was super excited to see what God might be up to with this couple. Well, they met for an hour and during that time, Dan laid out the gospel in detail and that couple prayed along with Dan to be saved. Hallelujah!

This couple that came in for counseling for their marriage, got that help, but they also got much bigger help than that. They got saved for eternity. They stayed at our church for a couple of years before moving. Praise be to the God who saves, even people who illegally drive through my driveway (Acts 9:18).

The principle

Churches often want to start a ministry to their community that will be *different*. Something new that isn't offered other places. They want to know if biblical counseling could be that ministry. One church in Ripon, California, came with just that question. There are lots of food banks out there and it seems every church reaches out to the homeless in some capacity.

But no one offered counseling to their little community. They wanted to know if I thought this would work out there. You can guess what I said.

After much prayer, they concluded they wanted to put their feet in the shallow end of the pool and start by showing their church what biblical counseling would look like. So, they brought me out there for an eight-week series. They thought maybe thirty to forty people would come. Well, seventy-five people came for eight weeks. These were super nice people who loved God and His Word. Being a farming community, and using their vernacular, they were ripe for the pickin'.

Well, fast forward to today and I can tell you that not only do they offer biblical counseling to their community, but they also have hired a full-time pastor who counsels and trains other counselors just like we do. And, they report the same thing: people are getting saved there, too. Again, praise be to God.

The bottom line is that what I've heard everywhere I've gone is that this is one of the most effective, if not the most effective ways to share the gospel that most churches have going.

How this can help your ministry

It should be obvious at this point but just in case, pastor, start counseling your people. You will be shocked how many people come to faith through this ministry. It may happen via an actual counseling situation like Peter and Mary or it may happen through the class you offer to your church like the one we offer at NorthCreek.

One of my counselors had been at NorthCreek for ten years, thinking he was a Christian. Through the biblical counseling class we call Cornerstone, he realized he was not saved until that class. He gave his life to Christ that year and became one of our counselors and still is, twenty years later. Again, praise be to God.

I know there are lots of events and programs out there that churches want to run for the purpose of evangelism. We love quick results. We love the idea of revivals. We love to be able to count how many got saved. I would just ask that you look at those numbers carefully and think about where those people are today. Then, I would ask that you consider investing long-term time and money into people who want to help you help other people. If

Lessons Learned

you're not a pastor, start helping him help people and then ask him to pray about expanding the ministry you are already doing.

I guess what I'm encouraging is, let go of the big flashy programs and start a biblical counseling ministry at your church.

Steve Mawhorter

Lessons Learned

Chapter 24

The power of prayer

(Lk. 18:1-18)

I wonder how often we pray for our friends, counselees, and congregants because we are supposed to pray. I wonder how often we are driven to pray. I wonder if we really believe that our prayers make a difference. I'd like to share two amazing stories of answered prayer that will teach you not to doubt the prayers you offer up to God on behalf of your people.

Meet Garry

The first one happened about 15 years ago. I have a history in the finance world. I was a day-trader in the 80s and 90s. It was a crazy business back then, so much more volatile than it is today. When you hear someone talk about the volatility in the markets today, just know that today's market swings are child's play compared to what I experienced back then.

Well, back in the 80s, I broke off from my company to start my own investment company with two other guys from the same firm. We needed an assistant. I knew someone that I thought would catch on very quickly and would be trustworthy. His name was Garry Pollard. I had only known Garry for two years but somehow I knew he would do well, and he did. I stayed with the company for 7 years before retiring. Garry stayed behind as a bond trader for another 8 years after that.

Garry and I were on parallel paths in ministry during the mid to late nineties into the early two-thousands. I was coaching basketball and teaching bible at a local Christian school as well starting and leading men's ministries and the biblical counseling ministry at NorthCreek Church. Garry was an elder but desiring to do more for the Lord.

One night, back in 2002, Garry and his wife Darcy had a discussion about their future. Garry was tired of the job and just plain tired in general from getting up at 4:30AM every day. Later that night, Garry prayed that God would give him something more fulfilling than working in the finance industry. Ready for this?

The very next day, Garry's boss, my ex-partner, laid him off. Yep, he laid him off. His reason? He just decided he didn't want to trade bonds anymore and since that is what Garry did, he no longer had any need for him. Nice prayer and interesting answer to Garry's prayer, right?

At first, Garry struggled with the answer. To say the least, it wasn't what he expected and it made him a little sad . . . until the next day. Garry was washing his car and listening to a sermon on the radio. The speaker said that God might even have to get you fired in order to get your attention. Well, God had gotten Garry's attention.

Within a few days, our senior pastor, Jon McNeff, came into my office and shared that he really needed an executive pastor/director. He asked me if I thought Garry could do the job. Knowing Garry's skill set as I did, that was a no brainer, absolutely. Within a week, Garry was hired as our new Executive Director, a position he held, along with being an elder, for the next 15 years. Nice answer to prayer, huh? Most of us wait years for an answer like that. Garry didn't have to wait a week.

Meet Chrissy

My second one involves my daughter, Chrissy. Chrissy was a student at The Master's College (TMC), majoring in Kinesiology. She was an athlete in high school and great in her science classes as well. She has an amazing memory. She figured she'd use both those interests and maybe go into sports training. Sounded good at the time, but the Lord had other plans. During her second year at TMC, something happened that is worth sharing in this book.

The school provided opportunities for their students to apply some of their training as an intern. It was during this time, that she realized that 90% of her time as an athletic trainer would be spent taping ankles and icing various body parts of sweaty, smelly football players. Maybe it was that or maybe it was because she used to get hit on by the athletes and then get lectured for distracting the boys. Either way, being a physical trainer was losing its appeal.

She shared this with her Resident Director, they prayed about it, and she quit. The very next day, something happened that can only be attributed to a "God-thing."

That previous summer, Chrissy had spent some time in Tanzania working for a center for children with disabilities. She saw how few resources there were. In fact, they didn't even have a sign language for the deaf. She thought then that maybe a job working with children with disabilities in other countries would fill a great need.

So, that next day, as she was walking through the parking lot at TMC, a school that is in the middle of a neighborhood, there was a woman who was passing out flyers on campus recruiting employees. Though there were other students around her, this woman looked Chrissy in the eye and asked if she knew anyone that would want to work with children with autism.

Hah, Chrissy thought! This is my answer to prayer. So, piecing together her experience in Tanzania, her experience with football players, and her prayer from the previous day, in a split second, she said, "how about me?" This totally came out of the blue. But the timing was such that I think she knew this must be from God. The woman said, "great, you're hired." Cool story so far, but there's more.

At the same time, there was a family who had a child with autism nearby. This was a family of believers. They attended Grace Community Church in Los Angeles, Dr. MacArthur's church. However, because of their child's autism, the husband and wife could never attend church together. One always had to stay home with him because even though there were parents at the church to help, the little boy couldn't tolerate it.

They had been praying for years for someone who could stay with their son while they attended church together. God answered their prayers with Chrissy. Fourteen years later, Chrissy had received her Bachelors, her Master's, her ABA (Applied Behavior Analyst) certificate, and her BCBA (board certified behavioral analyst). Oh, and she got married and had a baby at the same time. And, she is still serving families of children with autism.

Is that not an amazing story?

The principles

I learned a couple of things worth mentioning. The first one is the obvious one. God sometimes answers prayers right away. I think we all know that, but do we pray as if we know that? As pastors and counselors, it's easy to fall into the path of believing that if I just say all the right things in all the right ways, I can get people through their troubles and back into better places. That's a trap and very presumptuous on my part to think that. We need to pray and we need God to answer.

The second thing I learned requires a little more explanation from my own personal life. I remember several years ago, while I was praying with my wife, that I apologized to Him for coming back to Him with the same request over and over. When I finished praying that morning, my wife asked, "what was that all about? Why did you apologize for asking something from God?"

I was a bit tongue-tied with her question. This, by the way, is the way my wife counsels me and it's very effective. Ladies, you should try it sometime. She asks questions. Simple questions. It's very effective.

Well, my answer revealed that my prayer life had fallen into the category of thanksgiving and left requests behind. I had begun feeling guilty for asking for anything from God that was for me. I was fine asking for others but not for me. Her question and that moment changed me.

Ever since that time, my prayer life has become aggressive. I feel no shame in asking God for anything and everything. Even if I ask for the wrong thing at the wrong time, the Holy Spirit will take that prayer and make it right anyway (Rom. 8:26-27). So, I just cry out to God as numerous Psalms exemplify, and I throw them at God. Some of my prayers are quite greedy for people. I mean, I don't mind asking for miracles in people's lives. God's going to do what He wants anyway. My job is to cry out to Him and wait for Him to answer, expecting to see His goodness on display (Ps. 27). In fact, this past year, I threw ten major prayer requests at God. Nine were answered with an affirmative. Only one was a no. God is good all the time and all the time, God is good.

When you pray, do you think answered prayer is an isolated incident? Or, do you think that God is always at work in our lives, whether we see it or not? When you pray for your people, do you pray as if the answer is right around the corner? Do you believe it is or do you just hope that it is? Maybe you get a little weary of praying without seeing answers like these that I've just told you? Or, maybe you just feel bad because you go back to the same prayer over and over. Or, maybe you feel like God has already heard that prayer and is tired of hearing it. If that's the case, you should become more familiar with the Parable of the Unjust Judge, found in Luke 18:1-8. It says this,

Now He was telling them a parable to show that at all times they ought to pray and not to lose heart, ²saying, "In a certain city there was a judge who did not fear God and did not respect man. There was a widow in that city, and she kept coming to him, saying, 'Give me legal protection from my opponent.' For a while he was unwilling; but afterward he said to himself, 'Even though I do not fear God nor respect man, yet because this widow bothers me, I will give her legal protection, otherwise by continually coming she will wear me out.'" And the Lord said, "Hear what the unrighteous judge said; now, will not God bring about justice for His elect who cry to Him day and night, and will He delay long over them? I tell you that He will bring about justice for them quickly. However, when the Son of Man comes, will He find faith on the earth?"

How do you see God when you pray? Is He the one who is bothered by your prayers or is he the one who will not delay in answering?

How this can help your ministry

That day in prayer with my wife changed me. I hope that it does you, too. My encouragement to you in this chapter is to pray for your people, with your people, with great passion and expectation. God is all knowing, all powerful, all wise, perfectly loving, merciful, and gracious. He is good and does nothing but good. Pray for your people as if you believe this to be true, since it is, and look for it with them while you wait for His amazing goodness.

Lessons Learned
Chapter 25

Take the call! Make the call!

Meet Terry

Several years ago, while I was working on my ACBC certification and the church's certification as an official training center for ACBC, we got a call from a guy from Brownsville, Texas, Terry Hoskins. Terry had a B.S. in biblical studies and an M.S. in marriage and family therapy but was serving at a children's home on the Mexican border. Though an admirable job for anyone, he felt a little unsatisfied with that and wanted to do something more. He didn't know exactly what that would look like so he began making a few calls to biblical counseling centers throughout the country. When he googled "biblical counseling center," our name came up first. Keep in mind, we are 2,000 miles away from Brownsville where he was living.

When Terry called our office, my assistant took the call and listened to his story. Basically, she was screening my calls. After listening to Terry's story, she thought I should take the call. To my shame, I didn't want to do it. He called at a terrible time. I was knee deep in certifications, training, counseling, pastoring, etc., etc. I just didn't have time for some guy from Brownsville, Texas who didn't know what he wanted to do with his life. Shame on me, right? Shame on me.

Well, something happened inside me and I took the call. Maybe it was the Holy Spirit. Maybe it was just my assistant who sounded a lot like the Holy Spirit in that moment. Either way, I took the call from Terry. He explained his situation and I explained what biblical counseling is and how our ministry got where it was at that point. After 15 minutes, he sounded encouraged and that was it . . . so I thought.

A couple of years later, I'm at the annual ACBC Conference at Faith Church in Lafayette, Indiana. I'm in a workshop, sitting in a classroom, waiting for the speaker to begin, and out of the blue, some guy sitting next to me starts up a conversation. I looked at his name tag and guess who it is. Yep, it's Terry from Brownsville. He proceeded to tell me how he had started working on his certification with ACBC and was excited to see where God might be taking him. Good story, right? Well, it's not over.

A couple of years later, I'm on vacation in Marco Island, Florida, 3,000 miles from my home in Walnut Creek. It's Saturday night and my wife starts talking to me about where we might go to church on Sunday. As any good pastor would, I poopooed her idea. "You really think you'll find a decent church on this little vacation island? Well, you can try." I was sure there was no way she would find a solid church on this little vacation island.

Fifteen minutes later, she tells me she thinks she has a place that I'm going to like. Though suspicious, my curiosity was piqued. She showed me the website and would you believe this, they have a counseling center there and they say it's biblical. I'm thinking, "yeah, a lot of people call what they do *biblical* but it's anything but biblical. We'll see. So, the next day, we headed over to the church.

After the service, as we were headed out, I thought I should find whoever runs the counseling ministry and just say hello from California. After all, I am the director of one of the largest training centers in America, right. I felt a little obligated, but I had hoped I would at least see someone that I might someday see at an Annual ACBC conference. It might be a nice connection. Chances were that I'd meet someone from the church but probably not the person running the counseling center. But, hey, you never know, right?

So I found the welcome center, and guess who I find. Yep, it's the guy who is running the counseling center and it's Terry from Brownsville. He's running the show. And, fast forward a couple more years and guess what he's doing now. He's now the senior pastor of that church. Who knew?! Well, God did, so when someone calls you and you don't feel like taking the call, TAKE THE CALL.

How this can help your ministry

Now, maybe as you're reading this, you're thinking, "I'm more like Terry than you." You're the one needing some advice. Well, then, you make the call. You see, we need each other. Every one of us stands on the shoulders of someone else. I didn't invent what we do here. I didn't have a 10-year plan, a 5-year plan or even a 3-year plan. I took 1 year at a time, connecting with people around the country and around our community. At first, it was me and 5 women in our church counseling. In the greater bay area, there were only 2 other guys who were doing what we do. Now, 20 years later, there are over 125 churches doing what we do. That happened because people made uncomfortable calls to me and other people took calls they didn't have the time to take.

Folks, we all need each other. If you're the guy out there who feels like he's the only one on the island who wants to do biblical counseling, you're not. Be bold. Put one foot in front of the other. In faith, call people who you think probably don't want to talk to you. I can assure you, a few will not take your call because they think they are too busy with their ministry like I did. I can also assure you that most of the others, who are just as busy, who will take the call anyway and bless your socks off.

Steve Mawhorter

Section 3

Practical Wisdom for your Ministry

Lessons Learned

Chapter 26

Follow the cloud

(Ex. 13:21-22)

Our story at NorthCreek Church

NorthCreek Church, where I have been since 1984, is located in Walnut Creek, California. When I got here, we had a form of integrated counseling at our church. Anyone who needed counseling was referred out to this group. Fast forward to the date of this writing, 2019, and we now have a vibrant biblical counseling ministry with over sixty trained counselors who counsel over two hundred cases a year and that is in addition to all the counseling the pastors and elders do separate from the counseling ministry.

When I started the ministry, there were only 2 other churches in the greater bay area with a biblical counseling ministry. There are now over 125. When I tell people our story, everyone wants to know, "how did your church ministry grow like this?" What's your secret? Well, to use a biblical simile, I like to tell people that we just *followed the cloud*. Let me explain what I mean.

After 430 years in captivity, the Israelites had been released. Six hundred thousand men plus women and children. Yowzer, that's a lot of people! Upon release, they had many worries. Will the Egyptians come after us again? What will we eat? Where are we going? How do we get there?

Well, with the internet unavailable to them, the Lord provided his own form of Googlemaps in the form of a cloud. Exodus 13:21-22 reads, "The Lord was going before them in a pillar of cloud by day to lead them on the way, and in a pillar of fire by night to give them light, that they might travel by day and by night. He did not take away the pillar of cloud by day, nor the pillar of fire by night, from before the people." All they did was follow the cloud and that's all we have done at NorthCreek.

We didn't have a three-year, five-year, and ten-year plan. We didn't have targets to hit and goals to reach. We just wanted to help people help people. Though I don't have a game plan for you to follow you probably want, I do think you will benefit from the backstory as you follow your own cloud. Here's our story.

In 1995, and recently retired from the financial world, I sat down with our new Pastor, Jon McNeff, to see if he had any thoughts on how he could use me at NorthCreek Church. Pastor Jon offered me four different ministry options. None were appealing but I accepted the position of men's ministries leader, which I held for five years. However, one month after accepting the position, things changed.

On a trip to southern California, where I grew up, one of my friends from Youth For Christ reminded me that my dream as a young man was to make a lot of money young, retire, and be a counselor. Due to the Lord's grace in my life, I got those first two right, but I had completely forgotten the last one. As soon as my friend said that, the lightbulbs went off in my head like a Christmas tree and I knew, *this is why nothing Pastor Jon wanted me to do was appealing.*

I went back to Jon and told him I wanted to be a biblical counselor. What I didn't know was that Pastor Jon headed up the biblical counseling ministry at his previous church before he came to NorthCreek. We were both excited, and though we didn't talk about it this way, I think we both sensed the cloud was moving. Pastor Jon recommended that I get to work on my education and so I did.

I started my Masters' work in 1996 and got about a third of the way through, but the cloud moved again. Pastor Jon wanted to start small groups as well as the counseling ministry so, in 1997, we did a 13-week series for people who either wanted to be a small group leader or a counselor. He spoke the majority of the time, but I got to speak twice.

After the series was over, we split up. While seventy people continued on in the small group training, a grand total of 6 women followed me into the world of biblical counseling. I trained them that year with what I knew at the time, which wasn't much, and 5 of the 6 made it all the way through.

Then one day, while researching how to get us all certified, I came across International Association of Biblical Counselors (IABC). They fancied themselves as "the gentle voice for biblical counseling." I liked that line and could sense the cloud was moving again, so all 6 of us got certified with IABC.

That first year and a half of training was very significant for us as a team. We learned and were challenged at the same time. We all went to 2 conferences that summer of 1998, one with IABC and one with IBCD. We had a blast that summer. All we wanted to do was help a few people through troubled times. None of us knew what was in store for us down the road. We were all just following the cloud.

That next year, someone suggested we should offer the training out to the whole church as a training class on Sunday mornings so, following that cloud again, we did. In 1999, we started our first class and called it Biblical Counseling. Ingenious name, isn't it? So creative. That first class started with 17 people. We ended with 11, and 2 became counselors.

The next year, we started with 45 people and ended with 25, adding 2 more counselors. The next year, we started with 65 and ended with 45, adding more counselors. Do you see a pattern here?

Well, eventually we got a little more creative with the name of the class and renamed it *Cornerstone*, and the class continued to grow. We still offer this class, now on Wednesday evenings as part of our Wednesday evening programs. Routinely we have between 150 to 200 people attending. The class has been video recorded and is available on the church website, www.northcreek.org.

By 2005, we had taken 700 plus people through Cornerstone and had accumulated over 20 counselors, when another significant moment occurred. Again, this was another meeting with Pastor Jon and I having a pivotal conversation.

I had a hunger to take what we had created at NCC and repeat that at another church in another city where biblical counseling didn't exist. Pastor Jon said, "why do you have to leave to do that? Just do it here." I thought, *duh, why not?* So, I did. Here goes that cloud again.

I started meeting with other pastors in the area, and by *in the area*, I mean within a fifty-mile radius. I started meeting with and getting to know good, solid men, who loved God and His Word, and who loved the idea of biblical counseling. Within two years, we offered our first biblical counseling training, which has now come to be known as the NCT (NorthCreek Counseling Training).

That first one-day seminar brought together 100 people from 20 different churches. The next year, prompted by a call from one of the pastors at Faith Church in Lafayette, Indiana, we hooked up with them to bring their guys in to do our training.

They take their one-week training *On the Road*, as they call it, and do it in a 3-weekend format, one weekend per month, on a Friday and Saturday. We did a Fundamentals track for first-timers and an advanced track for everyone else. The first year using the guys from Faith, we had 140 people. The last year of three years, we had 260 people. After three years, we finished our time with them and then continued to run our own conferences, using the same format. We have now been running these conferences for 10 years in total. This last year, 2019, we had 650 people from over 120 churches and 60 full time pastors. People even come from other States.

Now, think about this for a minute. In 1998, there 2 other churches doing what we were trying to do. Now, 20 years later, there are well over 125 churches doing what we're doing. Can you believe that?! I can't.

As a church, we started with those 5 ladies who finished that first year. We counseled together for almost 15 years before people moved out of town or changed ministries. We have gone from those 5, counseling 20-30 cases a year, to over 60 counselors counseling over 200 cases per year.

In addition to that, we became a certified training center for ACBC (formerly known as NANC). We help other churches get their people certified with ACBC. To do that, we held a class that helps people get through the hardest part of the certification process: the exams. After seeing how helpful it was to so many people, I thought, *"hey, why not video record them,"* so we did. Those can be also be found on the church website. Again, just following the cloud here, just following the cloud.

Since that time, I have probably had 20 people, not from our church, tell me how thankful they were that we did this and that without those videos, they might not have made it through the certification process. And, with those 20 people, many of those are churches where those videos are playing to several people at a time. The videos have probably helped over 50 people through certification now.

Lessons Learned

I hope this chapter has not felt like bragging, because it's not. If there is any bragging, it's bragging about what God can do with just a few people who want to help a few more. We just put one foot in front of the other, year by year, and responded to ideas that various people came up with. There is of course more detail to this story. If you would like that, feel free to contact the church and ask for me, or you can just google my name. I'm not hard to find and I live to bring biblical counseling to the world. Call me.

Steve Mawhorter

Lessons Learned

Chapter 27

How to start a Biblical counseling ministry in your church

Nearly every month for a period of about 5-10 years, I would receive a call from a pastor wanting to start a counseling ministry in his church. Hoping to accomplish the same thing, they always want to know how we did what we have done at NorthCreek Church. I loved those meetings because I got to brag about the Lord but I also loved those meetings because I knew these men would follow through on what they heard and because I knew that, I knew that hundreds, in fact, even thousands more people are going to get some real help from their church.

These meetings not only helped those churches, but they also helped me think through more carefully how God did what He did here. Soon I was asked to present at the annual ACBC conference on the same topic, which again made think through how this all happened. That presentation led to me being asked to present this same material through the ministry of Overseas Instruction in Counseling (OIC) in 3 countries, the Philippines, Australia, Japan. I am now on the board for that ministry and hope to soon make similar presentations in other countries.

This chapter is meant to help you, the pastor or counselor, think through how you can replicate what we have done here at NorthCreek Church. From the following list of principles, take from it what is helpful. Trash the rest.

The principles

The first and most important point is to make sure your senior pastor, elder board and pastoral staff are all on board with the sufficiency of Scripture as it relates to growth, not just salvation. You probably think they already are, but I can tell you that all it takes is for one of those men to be funding his daughter's college education with her major being psychology and you may have a problem. If you're the senior pastor reading this, take the time to teach your staff and elders before you go telling your congregation that you now offer biblical counseling.

Second, find someone to champion the ministry, preferably a man. Why a man? Several reasons. One, he'll be doing a lot of teaching and you need a man to teach other men (1 Tim. 2:11-15). Two, it's easier to get more men when one a man is the recruiter. Three, much of your counseling is marriage counseling and for that, again, you'll need a man in the room to lead the way.

Third, the senior pastor, not someone who makes announcements, should announce to the congregation that the ministry has begun and who will be leading it. This tells the sheep that their senior pastor trusts this guy. He will have instant credibility with most of the church. The rest will come along over time. That's exactly what happened at our church. I remember asking my senior pastor why people would listen to me. He said, "because I'm going to tell them to." I said, "okay, I guess." Well, you know what? He was right and they did.

Four, the senior pastor needs to refer to this ministry from the pulpit in the sermons, not just announcements. He can just weave it into the fabric of his messages. For example, when he's teaching on marriage from Ephesians 5:22-33, he can just say something like this, "I know that there can be seasons in a marriage that can be difficult and you might be in one right now. If you are, contact the church and ask for biblical counseling. We have people there who are trained to help during this time." You think you'll get a few calls that week? Yes, you will.

Five, start training counselors. There is tons of great material out there. I trust you can find that on your own, but if not, contact ACBC, Faith Church in Lafayette, even us here at NorthCreek. The point is not where you get the material. The point is, train your people.

Six, find some other faithful men who desire to help people this way. I say "men" because you don't really have to try to find women. They will come to you. They are more inclined to be counselors anyway.

Seven, control your growth. Build with quality and go slow. Reputations are easy to make, good and bad, but bad ones are hard to break. So, take your time. Train them well. Don't make a cattle call announcement to your entire church that you are looking for people who want to be counselors. Look around. Who is naturally inclined this way? Who do people already go to without anyone asking them? These are the ones to start with. You can grow later. Right now, you just want to build with a few quality people.

Eight, give them cases that they can handle. Don't overwhelm them with the difficult cases. For example, don't assign them to someone who's just discovered their spouse is having an affair or the suicidal person or the anorexic cutter or the one who's been diagnosed with bipolar disorder. Those people are hard for all of us but for someone new, they'd be in way over their head and you'd be doing a disservice to your counselee. Give them someone who's boyfriend just broke up with them or a guy who's struggling with porn or woman is married to a lazy man. These are normal situations.

Nine, take your people to biblical counseling conferences. ACBC, CCEF do annual conferences in October every year. Faith Church does a weeklong conference in February. Several other churches do annual 3 weekend conferences over a 3-month period. NorthCreek does theirs in August to October. These are invaluable times of learning, fellowship, and bonding as your people learn how to help people, together.

Ten, after you have assigned counselees, meet with your counselors regularly. We started out meeting as a group. There were 5 counselors and me for about 5 years, meeting in a home or at church discussing cases without names. We all listened and prayed for our people together. We gave advice to each other and supported each other. Over time, as the ministry grew, those meetings became impossible to continue but they really set the tone for the first twenty years of ministry and it gave me personal contact with each one of them.

Eleven, develop a budget. If you're a small church, this will be difficult, I know. But, listen, your church needs to know that you value this ministry enough to fund part of it. We started super small. I think I was paid five thousand dollars that first year and I think I was given some money to help bring people to conferences. Eventually, I was given an assistant who was paid for ten hours of part-time help per week. You'll need this when you get to ten counselors. The point is, start somewhere and let it grow as the success of the ministry grows.

Twelve, decide on certification. People need to be trained before they are given people to counsel, but they do not need to be certified by an outside organization. You can do that in house if you have the resources. That said, certification by an outside organization will help the counselor know that she knows what she knows. And, it will help the counselees coming to you for your help if they know that these lay people have been through some rigor of professional training. Seeing those certifications on the wall will help with that. It takes time and money, but everyone will benefit by going through the certification process. There are lots of organizations out there that certifies counselors, but we have chosen to go with ACBC. I recommend the same to you.

Thirteen, build a good list of resources for your counselors and counselees. At NorthCreek, we have a great one and are happy to share that with you. These include books, articles, podcasts, even MP3s and downloads of all kinds.

Fourteen, get to know other churches and their ministry in the area and rob them of their experience and materials. We didn't get where we are by making it up. We all stand on the shoulders of someone else, don't we? Don't be shy. Ask.

Last, aim at being a church that thinks this way, not just a church that has a ministry that thinks this way. What you don't want is a church that has a counseling ministry and everyone who has a problem goes there. No, no. That's not how it's supposed to be. We are all called to be disciple-makers (2 Tim. 2:2), which is what counseling is. We are all called to love, encourage, strengthen, comfort, etc., one another (Rom. 15:14; 1 Thess. 5:14). Be a church where everyone thinks biblically about life. It will create unity in your church and together, everyone will be strengthened for greater usefulness to the Lord.

Folks, there is more to say on this topic than is permitted in this short book. Feel free to contact NorthCreek Church at any time. You can ask for me or you can ask for the Pastor of the ministry but do call us.

Lessons Learned

Chapter 28

How do I find people who can help me help my people?

(Matt. 25:21)

First, let me say that the fact that you are even reading this chapter, tells me that your heart is in the right place. You've already acknowledged you can't do it all and other people might be more gifted or appropriate than you are anyway. Well done. Now, how do you find people in your church that can help you help your people?

Well, before you go around looking for people, you need to know what it is that you're looking for in those people. Then, we can talk about how you can find them.

What you're looking for on a spiritual level

First, are they aligned with the Statement of Faith at your church, especially the inerrancy, authority, and sufficiency of Scripture? If they are not but they seem to have a heart for people, don't rule them out quite yet. Instruct them on these issues. See if you can win them. You may have a very valuable counselor who has just never really been taught.

We had one such woman in our church. She had a master's degree in psychology and was well put together, but she did not believe in the sufficiency of Scripture. In fact, she told me that one night, when I was teaching *Why you can't trust psychology*, that she got so angry that she kicked her book across the room. She left that night and didn't return. A year later, she was back. The Lord had changed her mind. She became one of our counselors for many years.

Second, are they growing in their faith and understanding of the Word (2 Pet. 3:18) and are they willing to put in the time required to be trained? We figure that our training takes about two hundred and forty hours, mostly reading and some writing.

Third, is their life characterized by a healthy submission to the Scriptures, the Holy Spirit, church leadership, and maybe even their small group leaders (Heb. 13:7, 17)?

Fourth, do they show a teachable spirit and a lifestyle of humility (1 Pet. 5:5)? I find that not only are the best counselees people who are humble and teachable but so are the counselors.

Fifth, does their giftedness match what is needed as a counselor? For example, the gift of administration and service are great gifts, but they are not necessarily the most needed in a counseling room. Your administrative assistant needs those gifts, but your counselors need to be gifted in things like mercy, encouragement, teaching, and so on.

What you're looking for on a practical level

First, are they around? I grew up with this acronym: FAT; faithful, available, and teachable (Matt. 25:21). I mean, when you offer a class, are they there? When you're preaching, do you see them in church. This is super practical but super helpful. Think of the opposite. You hardly see them and then they come to you and say they want to help you counsel your people. You might want to pass on them until you see them on a regular basis. Maybe give them another way they can serve and you can observe them from a distance.

Second, I also love people that are inquisitive. They ask great questions. You know those people in your class who often have things to say, but not questions to ask? Those people who think that you need help teaching your class? Those are not the people you need helping you counsel. They've already learned what they need to learn and they're more interested in being the talker/teacher than the learner and counselor. If they're good people and have shown a life of wisdom, you might want to spend a little more time with them personally training them, and make sure they really are ready to help you help people. In the meantime, look for those people who ask lots of questions.

Third, observe how they respond to people when people talk to them and observe how other people respond to them when they are talking. Are they good listeners or just good talkers? When they talk, do they talk non-stop? Do other people like talking to them or do people avoid them? I think you can learn a lot by just watching how other people interact with them.

Fourth, I like to look for people who are winsome. Perhaps I naturally look for that in others because that's the way that I am, but I think there's more to it than that. God is good all the time and all the time, God is good. So, no matter why the person is seeking your help, God is being good. He's up to something special with their lives. Even in some of the darkest times with my counselees, there is a little laughter. Faith is written all over my face and sometimes my faith is all the faith they have. There's much more I can say about winsomeness, but I'll leave it up to you think that through more for yourself.

Fifth, how is their family life? That must be in order. It does not have to be perfect, but it needs to be good and I mean really good. If there is disharmony or dissatisfaction somewhere in that marriage, you will eventually have a problem. Rather than being a counselor, this person needs to get some counsel first. In fact, you'll find that some of your better counselors were your counselees. I think about a third of our counselors were at some time counselees themselves, me included.

How do you go about finding them?

First, go before the Lord and ask. I would say even get on your knees and beg the Lord for good people that will help you help people. I believe that is the kind of prayer you can take to the bank. I went to God once about this.

We were in desperate need of more men as counselors. Our waitlist just kept growing and growing. We even had to stop taking new counselees for a time. We had plenty of women but there was only three other men that could help me so that when we had a marriage problem, we didn't have the manpower needed. So, I called out to God, and did what I would NOT recommend you do. I put an announcement in the bulletin saying we were looking for men who wanted to help us counsel. That week, four men responded. Two of them were in their seventies, one in his fifties, and one in his late thirties. All four went through the counseling training for over a year and each ended up being a valued counselor for many years. Pray and then go do something.

Second, and another word on prayer. If you see some people who you think might have the goods for this but just aren't quite ready, start praying for them. Don't tell them you're praying that they will become counselors. That may awaken something that should be kept asleep. Instead, pray on your own that you will see them around more often, or that you'll start hearing about them from others. Pray that God will strengthen them and guide them into the area of ministry that they are best suited for, whatever that is.

Third, look for people with desire. The Scripture tells us that for an elder to be an elder, he must first have a desire to be one. I think we can learn something from that. I know that all are called to counsel one another. I fully believe that. But I also believe that some people are just better suited for it than others. Being a counselor, in an office, behind a desk, is not equally suited for everyone any more than all people being equally suited for setting up chairs. Counseling is a difficult, gut wrenching, heartbreaking task at times. It is definitely not for everyone.

You might see something in a person that tells you they would be great at this and you might even be right. But, if God has not put that desire in them, don't you go putting that desire in them. They may in fact end up on your counseling team someday, but for many possible reasons, this may not be right time for them. I'm saying, look for them, but don't chase them down. Let them come.

So, what do you do then when you observe someone that you think would make an excellent counselor? Wait. Pray for them and wait. If they come forward, that is a great time for you to tell them that you've been hoping they would come forward. Tell them what you have observed over the years and then give them a game plan going forward.

I know that some of you might be having a hard time believing that anyone will show up but hear me out. What I'm describing to you is the way we have done it and we have trained over seventy-five people and over sixty of them are still counseling. Trust me. It works.

Four final considerations

First, consider Deuteronomy 6:6, Colossians 3:16, 2 Tim. 2:15. Is the Word of God in their hearts? Does it naturally pour out of their mouths? The man that discipled me was like that. Al Siebert, with Youth For Christ, not only led me to Christ but he discipled me for 8 years in total. I owe much of my love of Christ, and my style of ministry to this man. With Al, you couldn't spend more than 5 minutes with him before the name of Jesus would come up. He's unique, I know, but this is how your people ought to be. The Word should naturally flow like a waterfall in Lake Tahoe, swiftly, easily, and year 'round.

Second, we read in Romans 15:14, that believers who are full of goodness and are filled with knowledge are able to admonish other people. Look for good people that are good and love to do good. And, look for people who are knowledgeable. They don't have to have all the answers to the end of times. They don't need to know how to explain the minor prophets or even the major prophets, though there is much richness there to be learned. They don't even need to know the origin of sin. They do however need to know God at a deep level, and they do need to know how to help people through His Word.

Third, are they sensitive to their own sin (Heb. 5:14)? Some people are either unaware and oblivious or impervious and uncaring. Whatever the reason, biblical counselors ought to be well aware of their own sinfulness before they go around trying to help other people through their issues. Jesus said it plainly, "…take the log out of your own eye, and then you will see clearly to take the speck out of your brother's eye (Matt. 7:5)." They don't have to be perfect, but they do have to aware of it, sensitive to it, and aiming at killing it.

Fourth, do they value the great commandment and commission as you do and your church does (Matt. 22:37, 28:18-20)? If not, find someone else.

Last, among others not mentioned, are they a good example to others (Titus 2:7-10)? Have they shown some perseverance in difficult situations? We have people on our counseling staff who have lost family members, children, and marriages. The fact is, I'll bet you that every one of our counselors has been through trying times and come through it with flying colors.

In conclusion, if the Word is in their heart, their faith is strong, their walk is right, and their values match yours, then as the fishermen say, "fish on!"

That means you have a good one on your hands. Train them and turn them loose.

Lessons Learned

Chapter 29

There's a limit

I want to address a topic that I have been asked about many times. How many counselees should you counsel at a time?

Recently, I had a conversation with a very good pastor friend of mine who shared with me that his newly hired counseling pastor for their new and thriving counseling ministry had taken on what they thought were too many counselees at one time. By the time we had our conversation, they had cut him down from a number in the twenties to a number in the high teens. I about gagged.

You see, when I first started counseling, my senior pastor advised that I take on no more than two or three counselees at one time. That was good counsel and I should have listened to it. The problem is, the needs are so great that it is near impossible to stick to that number. And, I didn't.

I told myself that my life situation, kids grown and gone, allowed me the time to take on more than most people. Additionally, I am the kind of person who manages stress very well. I was a day-trader in the financial markets for fifteen years prior to full time ministry. If you're not sure what that is, think of the movie *Trading Places* with Eddie Murphy and Dan Ackroyd. Literally, my net worth was at risk 24/7 for years. If I could handle that, I could handle a few people's problems, right?

Well, that was true. I could handle a few. And, then, I could handle a few more. I let myself get up to eight at one time. I told myself that it's not really eight meetings every week. It was more like four to five per week because many of my clients could not meet every week, so, being a numbers guy, I could handle eight. However, there's more to it than just numbers and life situations.

As the years went on, the kinds of cases I was taking began to change. Our ministry and influence in the area was growing such that if there was a difficult case at another church, we got the call. And, within our own church, if there was a difficult case, I got most of them. Then, the cases we were getting were not only growing in number but growing in difficulty as word got out that we were "the experts." I say that tongue in cheek because we are not experts. Experienced, yes. Experts, no.

So, as the number of cases grew and the number of difficult cases grew with it, my load began to change. Rarely did I get the easy ones. The notion of two to three cases of normal counseling cases was long gone. We were deep into a ton of difficult situations and I had accumulated most of those. I learned the hard way that there is a different kind of limit that one can take but I only learned it after the limit slammed me. It affected me socially, mentally, spiritually, and physically.

Being at a large church for over 30 years, we have accumulated a ton of lifelong friends. We have all have raised our children, seen some come to Christ, seen some fall away from Christ, and even buried some. We've seen marriages and divorces. We vacationed together, served in church together, worshiped side by side, and clung to each other during hard times. However, as I was accumulating these difficult cases, we spent less and less time with them because I was spending more and more time doing ministry.

Mentally, while our social life suffered, I began to spend an inordinate amount of time thinking about the cases and what I could do to fix them. It wasn't the only thing I thought about, but boy did I think about it a lot. I'd go to bed thinking about it and wake up thinking about it. I wasn't worried. I just wanted to figure out how to fix the problems people had.

Emotionally, though I didn't realize it, I started finding myself more emotional than usual. I'm already a little soft-hearted and sentimental. Choking up while watching a Hallmark movie is one thing, but choking up while watching The Wonder Years is another. I can't believe I'm admitting I like Hallmark movies!

And then, it hit me physically. By the end of a day, I'd give a big sigh as I laid down to try and sleep. But even though I would be exhausted, I'd wake up at odd hours and not be able to get back to sleep. Then, I started having dizzy spells. I'd be walking and I'd lean to the left. I'd turn over in bed or get up too quick and the room would spin. The last episode I had, I leaned so bad to the right as I walked that had I not been leaning on my wife, I would have fallen into the wall. When that happened, I knew that was it. I had to get this checked out.

We had all the tests done. They checked my brain to see if there was anything there and yes, as I've heard before, there was nothing there. Wink, wink. No tumor is what I mean. They checked my carotid arteries to see if they were clear and they were. They put a Holter monitor on me for 30 days and nothing showed up there either. And, of course, they did a full blood workup. Nothing showed up anywhere. Physically, I was fine. So, what was wrong.

A few months after these events had gone, I was preparing to preach a sermon on waiting on the Lord, from Psalm 27. As I was preparing my sermon, I started wondering how many cases I had been dealing with during the last two years and what kinds of cases those were. I was shocked at what I found. I had taken on more than twenty cases, most of which involved domestic violence, drugs and alcohol, and unfaithfulness in its many forms (porn to adultery). People, that's too much for anyone and it finally go to me. And, by the way, just so you know, at the time of this writing, it's been about a year since these cases finished. And, guess what? No dizzy spells. Interesting, huh? I guess the financial stress of being a day-trader is different than the emotional stress experienced by being a pastor who loves his people. I learned my lesson.

How this can help your ministry

My lesson to you in all this is for you to not only think through how many cases you are involved with but what kinds of cases you are involved with. Protect yourself. Protect your future counselees. Protect your counselors. If you're a pastor, maybe you can take one or two hard cases at one time. If you are a volunteer, one, maybe two, is all you can take at one time. When the Bible says to bear one another's burdens, it isn't saying that you should bear all the burdens. It's saying the body, in its entirety should be carrying the burdens together. Let someone else help you. Don't do it all yourself, or you won't make it.

Jesus had thousands of followers, hundreds of disciples, twelve super serious disciples (well, eleven), but he was very close to only three in particular. Though this is descriptive and not prescriptive, perhaps there is a lesson here that should be considered.

Lessons Learned

Chapter 30

Sometimes, it's going to get personal

(Phil. 1:8)

As you have already read in a previous chapter, the world tells you to keep your distance from people. They say, "don't let them attach and don't let yourself get attached to them." But, is that biblical? Is that really the way God wants us to be, unattached, unemotional, and disconnected? Where does mercy fit into that picture? What about bearing up with one another? Sheesh, what about just plain love? Aren't we supposed to love our brother/sister?

Well, I think over time that you are going to learn that what we do as biblical counselors is very different than what the world does, and it should be. While their goal is to avoid pain, ours is to love and to take on some of the pain others experience, but listen, it's going to cost you.

Being a pastor or counselor is much like being a parent and no one knows what it feels like to love your child except you, the parent. In the same way, no one knows what it feels like to love your congregation the way a pastor does, except the pastor/counselor himself. I think we can learn a lot about this from one person in particular in the Bible.

I know that Jesus is the perfect example for everything, but for several reasons, I want to use Paul as my example of what it looks like or feels like to be a pastor who loves his people.

We usually think of Paul as an evangelist. I mean, he did evangelize the world, so that's a pretty good thought. Or, we think of him as a bit of a Brainiac. His long run-on sentences, written like a lawyer, probably steer us that way. His arguments in the text are well ordered and his vocabulary very specific, so seeing him as a Brainiac makes sense, too.

We probably think of Paul as this man who suffered greatly as he traveled the world spreading the gospel and for good reason (2 Cor. 11:23-28). And, last, we think of Paul as an apostle and defender of truth. These are all true, but do we think of Paul as a lover of his people? I'd like you to see that part of Paul's person from the text in the hopes that it guides you into loving people the way he did.

Meet Paul, the lover

I'd like to show this different side of Paul by simply noting from the text itself. If you spend a little time going through every book he has written in the Bible, you'll see his love for his people expressed in 8 ways: his attitude towards his own lack of self-importance, his use of familial terms when speaking of his disciples, his affection towards them, his prayers for them, his hard work on their behalf, his suffering, his joy in their growth, and in his instruction. I'll go through these quickly, but I also recommend you spend more time on your own on this one.

First, we see Paul's love in his attitude towards his own lack of self-importance. In Acts 20:24, Paul says, "I do not account my life of any value nor as precious to myself." In Philippians 2:3-4, he says, "Do nothing from selfishness or empty conceit, but with humility of mind regard one another as more important than yourselves." In other words, *I am not important. You are.* In Romans 12:3, he writes, "For through the grace given to me I say to everyone among you not to think more highly of himself than he ought to think." Obviously, we all tend to think too highly or too often of ourselves.

Had Paul considered the value of his own life, his own self-image, his own self-esteem of any importance, how would the gospel have spread? He cared little to nothing about his own feelings of pain or hurt and gave himself to his people.

Second, we see Paul's love in the use of familial phrases like son, mother, brother, children. In 1 Cor. 4:17, he publicly identifies Timothy as his child. He calls the church in Galatia, his children (Gal. 4:19). In all 3 epistles known as the pastoral epistles, he identifies Timothy again as his child (1 Tim. 1:18, 2 Tim. 1:2, Tit. 1:4). In 1 Thess. 2:7-8, he says he cared for them with the gentility of a nursing mother. He says he has a fond affection for them and they have become very dear to him. Did you know that your pastor feels this way about you?

Do you think of your counselees as your children or you as a mother or father? Are they that dear to you? For Paul, his people were his family. Is that true for you? Do you they become like family to you or do you follow the world's instructions and hold them at arm's length, hoping not to get hurt?

Third, we see Paul's love in his affection. In Phil. 1:8, he says that he longs for them with affection, the affection of a mother. To Timothy, he wrote the he was hoping to come to him soon (1 Tim. 3:14). "For God is my witness, how I long for you all with the affection of Christ Jesus (Phil. 1:8)." To the church in Thessalonica, he described his affection as fond. To Philemon, he says he is sending his very heart (Phil. 12). Do you normally think of Paul, the defender of truth as this soft, affectionate guy?

Is this your heart for your people? Do you long to see them? Do you feel that kind of affection? Do you feel like their parents? I will say that at 39 when I first started counseling adults, I did not. Maybe, I was wasn't old enough yet to feel that way yet, but at 62 now, I do. Without question, they (the counselees) are my babies. I feel various levels of affection for them and often feel the weight of responsibility, that of a parent. This is not easy work people.

Fourth, we see Paul's love in his prayers for them. Paul writes that he doesn't cease in giving thanks for them when he prays (Eph. 1:15-16; 1 Thess. 1:11); he gets on his knees for them (Eph. 3:14); he prays for their growth (Col. 1:3,9); he prays that God will comfort and strengthen their hearts (2 Thess. 2:16-17); and he prays that they will experience joy, day and night (2 Tim. 1:3-4). Being a counselor or pastor is being a prayer warrior. Get on your knees for them.

I don't believe it's possible to pray for someone like this and keep them at arm's length. Through prayer, Paul's people were carefully woven into the fabric of his very soul. It sounds to me like he developed some pretty strong attachments. What do you think?

Fifth, we see Paul's love in his work. He sees himself as a tireless worker on behalf of his people using words like labor, which is agony in the Greek, (Gal. 4:19; Col. 1:28-29), striving (Col. 1:28-29; 1 Tim. 4:10), and serving (2 Tim. 1:3-4). Do you work this hard for people?

Sixth, we see Paul's love in his suffering. Anyone else you know received forty lashes for you? Consider the list of sufferings in 2 Cor. 11:23-29. Yet he says, "apart from other things, there is the daily pressure on me of my anxiety for all the churches." Not only is he willing to suffer but he calls on us to join with him in that suffering (2 Tim. 1:8; 2 Tim. 2:3). That's slightly different than what the world is saying to us, isn't it? God calls us to not only *not avoid suffering* but to embrace it, to join in on the fun, so to speak. Rather than to run from it, he calls us to endure it with him (2 Tim. 2:10) and with each other.

Seventh, we see Paul's love in the tie of his own joy with their growth. To the church he loved in Philippi, he indicates that his joy would be incomplete without the unity of the people in the church (Phil. 2:1-2). He later writes that they are his joy and crown (Phil. 4:1) and that he speaks proudly of the people in Thessalonica (2 Thess. 1:3-4).

Yes, part of Paul's joy was tied to the joy of the people he served and loved. That's how it is folks. We are inextricably linked to each other, connected by the blood of Christ and willing to spill it when called upon to do so. When they are happy, we are happier. When they are unhappy, we are less happy. I've heard it said and found it to be true that a parent is only as happy as his most unhappy child. The same goes for a pastor and that's okay.

Now, don't go all biblical on me and quote James 1:2-4, "consider it all joy my brothers . . . " I know the verse. It's written for a reason. Life is hard and when life is hard for others, their hardness will creep over into your hardness. That's just how it is and since it was good enough for Paul, it will be good enough for me and I hope it's good enough for you.

Last, we see it in his instruction. He says his goal is love from a pure heart and a good conscience and a sincere faith (1 Tim. 1:5). He sincerely loves his people. They are not projects or problems to fix. They are people to love.

How this can help your ministry

So, there you have it from the life of Paul. Is there any doubt that he was a lover of people? I love what John Piper says about Paul, "But in spite of the complexity and profundity of his thought, the balance and humanity of the man shines through the depth and tenderness and intensity of his emotions which (like his own imperfections) he is not hesitant to reveal."

What we do as biblical counselors is what Paul did for his people. We do not need to consider the world's notion of keeping your distance as worth spending one minute on. Reject it. Love your people the way you see Jesus and Paul loving people in the Bible.

How can you love people and keep your distance? You can't. Don't keep your distance. Climb boldly into their lives and love them deeply or fervently as Peter put it (1 Pet. 1:22). Connect with them. Hurt with and for them. Bond emotionally. There, I said it. Bond with your peeps.

Now, I say that with a great sense of confidence, but also one of fear. You are going to get hurt in doing this. I have been hurt a few times and will again. It isn't fun and it does hurt, and it will hurt again, but my goal is not to keep from getting hurt. My goal is to love people and I'm pretty sure that's what Jesus said to do, right (Matt 22:37-39)? Love Him and love others?

Listen, if you're goal is to help people without getting hurt, forget it. Don't bother. You're going to hurt for them, from the day they come in, and occasionally, you are even going to get hurt by them. It's just like having kids, isn't it?

When we had our kids, no one ever told us how hard it was going to be. We thought it would be mostly fun and games. Much of the time it was. However, much of the time it wasn't. Knowing what we know now, and how painful it can be as a parent, does that mean that if we did it all over again, we would never have kids? No. We'd still do it because we are called by God to do it. I would make the same case for counseling.

We are called to love people this way. I just don't want you to go in and expect it to be all peaches and cream. In one of the most famous quotes in a Hollywood movies, Tom Hanks, playing famously Forrest Gump said, "Life is a box of chocolates. You never know what you're going to get." True, isn't it? In counseling, you just never know what you're going to get.

Usually around Christmas time, one of our church members will bring a large box of See's Candies. I love Scotchmallows (dark chocolate, marshmallow and caramel). Those are the first to go, usually into my drawer. Within a couple of days, all the candy in this large box is gone except this one piece, called a Vanilla Nut Caramel. That's true every year. Everyone takes the good stuff first and leaves the bad stuff behind.

Counseling can be like this. All counselors want the Scotchmallow counselees and would prefer to leave the vanilla nut caramel counselees behind. Some are just more fun to counsel than others. You'll like some more than others. When it's over, some will leave a good taste in your mouth and some will leave a bad taste. All I can say is that it's a good thing Jesus and Paul didn't pick and choose their favorites because I doubt I would have been one of them myself. What would you be, a Scotchmallow or a Vanilla Nut Caramel?

Folks, God calls you to love everyone who comes to you for help. Love them. Get close to them. Hurt with them. Hurt for them. Be hurt by them. You'll get over it. But, if you just can't bear to be hurt, please do something else in the church. There are plenty of other places in the church where you can be used.

I'm not sure this chapter accomplishes all I intended but at a minimum, I do hope you have gotten a peak into your pastor's heart. He loves you like you are his child. If you've been a counselee, this is how much your counselor (hopefully) has loved you. Thank them for it, praise God for it, and then pass on that love to someone else.

Lessons Learned

Chapter 31

Don't do it!

Meet Brian

Brian was a small-town pastor with a small-town church. He was a one man show there. He did the music, the preaching, all the funerals and weddings. And, yes, he did the counseling. According to LifeWay Research, the average weekend attendance now in most churches in America is 80 people. That means, half of the pastors reading this chapter have the same dilemma that Brian had. What do you do when a woman comes to you for counsel?

Well, first let me say this. The Bible neither condemns nor advises pastors to counsel women or not to counsel women. Having been to many conferences over the years, it's almost universal that we are told not to counsel women. No specifics are given and though bible passages are thrown out at us, those verses aren't really written to answer this question at hand.

Second, though most of my instructors over the years have recommended against it, this has not been a universal answer. Some say, "that it's impractical to think you can never counsel a woman. You just have to show some discretion." So, which is it? Never? Or, just show some discretion? Before answering that, we need to consider what's behind these questions.

What's mostly behind the counsel that says "never counsel a woman" is that we fear, and for good reasons, that if a man counsels a woman, they will end up in an affair. This is a warranted fear. In fact, I would say it may be more warranted in the church than in the secular community. What I've written below will shed some light on the reasons for my opinion and if you're that one-man pastor like Brian, I'll give you some ideas on what to do for your ladies who need some help.

Before I go any further, let's just be clear. I am talking about whether a man should ever allow himself to meet alone with a woman on a regular, consistent basis for the purpose of giving her counsel. I am not talking about a one-time meeting or a once a year meeting. As a pastor, one-time meetings with a woman may be absolutely necessary and right (consider domestic abuse as an example) but ongoing, personal, regular, and consistent counsel is not necessary and can be dangerous to both her and to you.

Five reasons you shouldn't, just for her benefit

It's been said that sixty percent of all church attendees in solid bible teaching churches are women. So, right off the bat, nearly half of your women are either married to unbelieving men or single and very possibly lonely for the attention of a man.

Now, of the women who are married to believers, how many of those women feel loved by their husbands? How many of those marriages do you think are on solid ground? How many men have you counseled that really understand how to love a woman? How many of them even read their bibles on a daily basis? I suggest to you that there are very few, which means you have a lot of vulnerable women in your churches and why is that?

Most men are busy trying to put food on the table and a roof over their head. With what little energy they have left at the end of the day, it is spent on putting the kids to bed. By the time they're down for the night, their wives are ready for sleep. She goes to bed feeling disconnected. He goes to bed exhausted and probably sexually lonely. Folks, that's the majority of marriages today.

The women realize this is a problem and want to do something about it, but their husbands shrug it off. Men think, "we just need to have more sex." Women think, "Sex? Don't we need to talk more before having sex?" Marriages like this are in trouble, right? She wants help and wants to go to the pastor. He wants more sex and is uninterested in going to the pastor with his personal problems when they can all be fixed with a little more sex. Oh, brother!

On Sunday morning, you give a great sermon. Her heart is provoked and she calls you for help. Now, what! What are you going to do? Well, before you meet with her, consider a few things.

First, this is a woman who is emotionally disconnected from her husband. She is lonely for conversation. She wants to know what's going on in his life.

What does he think about? How does he feel about life? Where's he at spiritually? When you meet with her, you'll be talking and sharing with her in a way that she longs for with her husband but instead, it's with you.

Second, most Christian women long for a man who will connect with her spiritually. That means, he leads the way to regular church attendance. He pursues worship throughout the week. He regularly reads his bible and it is reflected in his life. He regularly prays by himself and, on occasion, he prays with her too. When he prays, he prays deeply. Her heart trusts in him because she can see and hear that he is fully connected to the Lord. Pastor, in her mind, you are that kind of man and now when you meet with her and she hears you pray. Can you see the danger in that?

Third, any hurting woman is longing for someone to show her some compassion and being a pastor, you know you must be compassionate. Read the gospel of Mark and make a note of every time you see Jesus being compassionate. It's throughout the book. You know that and so you are naturally compassionate with her. What do you think is going on in her head? Do you think she enjoys that? Do you think she wishes her husband were just a little more like you?

Fourth, and here's a crazy one for you. Since the advent in brain scans, studies are now showing that the same area of the brain that is activated by religious and spiritual experiences is also activated by sex and love. This explains why affairs involving pastors have begun while counseling their people. To illustrate, I'll get a little personal with you.

This is on a much lesser scale, but I can remember when I was twenty, my girlfriend and I would spend time going over a good religious book. We'd spend an hour talking about it. Then, I would pray. It was a sweet time. Guess what was next on the agenda and I mean immediately next? Yep, you got it. We made out and it was awesome. It was wrong, but it was awesome. This is how our bodies, specifically our brains, are wired. I didn't know this then, but I know it now and so do you. Don't be a fool. This is how we are all wired. Stay away.

The last one is the attraction issue. You might be thinking you're too old or too young or you're too fat or you're too short. Hey, maybe you're all three, old, short and fat. Maybe on top of all that, you're even bald. Men, it doesn't matter. She may not end up with you but her experience with you may open her mind to other men who are not old, short, bald and fat. You don't know exactly what's going on in her mind, but something is. Take responsibility.

Three reasons you shouldn't, for your benefit

I know what a lot of you are thinking. You're thinking, for a variety of reasons, I would never be attracted to her. My answer to that is this: If I put you on an island with her for six months and it's just the two of you, I'll bet dollars to donuts that sooner or later, you'll end up shacking up. The desire for sex is just too strong.

She may not be attractive to you now, but over time, her personality will become sweeter to you. You'll see her best, which is not what her husband sees, but you'll see it. She'll be kind, sweet, gentle, fun, soft, and so on. And, through those times together, you'll become attracted to the person inside the shell of that body and face. She may not have been attractive before, but that will change. You'll see that attraction is more about the heart than the body. And, if she makes a move towards you, look out.

As I mentioned in another chapter, one of my counselors said something hilarious to me. She said this, "men are no match for a woman. If she wants it, she'll get it. And, there's nothing they can do about it." When I heard this, I nearly fell of my chair in hysterics. Now, before I go on, she was talking about the world she came out of, the unbelieving, partying crowd, not the church. While I agree there's a difference, there is also a striking similarity.

We are all human. We are all material and immaterial beings. Our immaterial side, the heart or soul of every pastor is with the Lord. But, our material side, our flesh with its sexual cravings, is not always with the Lord. Come on, men. Just admit it. You're just as human as the man in the back row of your church. And, because of that, you are just as able to fall as he is.

If you are connecting with a woman in your church by counseling her or even with her, if she ever lays a hand on you, you'd better watch out. You just don't know when something might trigger something else and before you know it, you're in big trouble. Okay, enough of that topic. You get the point.

Here's a second reason you should stay away. You'll lose your bias. You see, not only will she become more attractive, she will become more convincing. Her husband is not there to explain himself. He's not there telling you how mean or demeaning she can be. You're getting all her good and he gets all the bad at home. You feel bad for her now but if you spent some time with him in his home, you'd feel bad for him, too. Because you're not there to see her in action, you just can't feel the same way about him as you do her and your advice will reflect that.

I'll give you one last reason to avoid this meeting. You are setting an example for the rest of your staff to follow and maybe you wouldn't fall but what about them? Can you say with the same confidence that they wouldn't either? How do you know that? Do you really know them the way you think you do? Do you really know what's going in their marriages? I would suggest you are best to assume you do not and that for the same reasons you should avoid it, they should as well. So, don't do it.

How this can help your ministry

This is fairly simple. First, when she calls, if she really needs help and you're the only game in town or even the best game in town, have a woman present with you. Perhaps she will have someone she can bring or perhaps you have someone in mind already. And, if that is not possible, have a woman in the loop, preferably your wife. Let her know about your meetings and what you are talking about. She will think clearly for you. She'll know when the lines are being crossed.

If you're single man, you shouldn't be handling this anyway, but if you must, an elder should be in the loop on this. You should be giving an account for every meeting you have with her, when and where and how long and what you're talking about. This can be of great advantage to her husband, too, because the elder may be able to reach out to him and get his involvement. In any case, you need the accountability. And, one more thing, if you ever have a meeting with this woman and you do not tell him, you are already in trouble. Get out.

Second, train some women in your church. They are more suited to counsel other women anyway (Titus 2:3-5). Women who want to help other women are not hard to find. Two-thirds of the people that come for counseling are women and guess what, about two thirds of our counselors are also women. That's just God's economy. Go with it. Train one. Then, train another one. You'll stay out of trouble and so will the vulnerable women that are coming to you for help.

Lessons Learned

Chapter 32

When do you cut 'em loose?

The question is often asked, "how do I know when to end the counseling relationship? How do I know when it's over?" Well, first of all there are two types of people: the ones who are doing well and growing, and the ones who are not doing well and are not growing. Let's handle both.

Meet Jerry and Melinda

Jerry was a young guy who had been struggling with pornography. It started when he was 12 but only occasionally. It really heated up when he went off to college where he found the freedom to pursue his fleshly desires. Upon graduation and returning home, he was hoping a change of scenery would help him get rid of this sin. It did for a while, but it soon returned. Within months, church began to take a backseat; his Bible got left on the shelf to collect dust; and he pretty much disappeared from fellowship. That's when he came to me. We met for a few months and he did very well. Jerry moved on and is now married.

Melinda, however, was a different story. She was married with kids but married to an unbeliever. She struggled with many things. She was depressed. She struggled with anger. She didn't like her husband and her children were difficult to raise because she and her husband could not get on the same page with how to raise children. She was a church-goer but not engaged in the life of the body. She had never served anywhere because her husband already complained about her being gone on Sundays for church. She was familiar with the Bible, but maybe only at a fifth-grade level. Melinda developed a nice relationship with her counselor, so much so that neither really wanted to end it.

This is the tale of two relationships and how men and women treat the counseling relationships different. For men, counseling is about fixing a problem and when that is done, the relationship is over, and they are ready to move on to another counselee.

For many female counselors, they tend to see counseling as a path to a relationship. This is not bad. In fact, it's great. Part of being a woman is being relational, more relational than men. However, it can create a little problem on the administrative/ministerial side. You see, the problem I have observed over the years is that while they are enjoying their new relationship, the waitlist for new counselees is growing. And, since we always have a waitlist at NorthCreek, it's a problem, but it's a solvable problem. The ladies just need to be encouraged to move their counseling along so they can get to another one.

Questions to ask yourself

When you're thinking about how to move people along, or cut 'em loose as the chapter is titled, there are a few questions that I ask myself. First, have I seen significant change in their actions and attitudes? What's significant, you ask? Good question. There's no blanket answer to that question. Just pray and ask God if there has been significant enough change to move them along.

Second, are they in the Word regularly? What's regular, right? I emphasize daily but I realize that is nearly impossible so if I can get them in the Word at least five times per week, I feel really good about that.

Third, are they in church regularly? This one's quite a bit easier to identify. Regular means every week unless they are out of town on vacation or at home with a sick child. This does not mean they also come to our midweek programs, though that would be excellent.

Fourth, are they worshiping regularly? This happens of course at church, but it also can happen in the car or at home. With modern technology the way that it is, we have access to music all the time everywhere we go. Is your counselee creating environments where the Word is not only read but listened to and even sung along with?

Fifth, when counseling is over, we want to make sure that people have found a place to serve before we move them on. This one is an easy one. People love to serve.

Lessons Learned

Last, a very good rule of thumb for me has to do with their heart idolatries. If you're not sure what that is, I recommend you read *Gospel Treason* by Brad Bigney. He does an excellent job explaining what heart idolatry is and how you help them figure out what that is.

The way I handle that is simple. I just ask them, "What would you say has been the ruling desires in your life that has gotten you into trouble?" If they have to search their brain longer than two seconds, we're not done counseling. It should be right on the tip of their tongue. However, if they do know it and they've shown an understanding of what to replace that with and how, I feel much better about releasing them.

Back to Jerry and Melinda, if you asked each of them those 6 questions, you'd have gotten excellent answers. The difference was, I was done with Jerry in 3 months. With Melinda, she and her counselor were going on 6 months. It was time for Melinda to move on. I know that this time horizon seems a little ambiguous, and it is, but you have to put some kind of limit on it, don't you?

Okay, this all sounds fine if your counselee is doing well, but what if your counselee is *not* doing well? What if they're not doing homework? What if instructions you give them goes in one ear and out the other?

I'll start with the least common situation—they do the homework but you're not seeing change. I've met with a few couples like this. We've met for six months. They do the homework, in fact, they're great at it. They gobble up every book I give them like it's Thanksgiving. They're in church and even serving. The problem is, I'm not seeing much change in the way they treat each other. This is rare, folks, but it does happen. So, when do you cut 'em loose?

Well, there's no black and white answer on this one but a decent rule of thumb on this, which I don't use, is four sessions. When talking to senior pastors, you'll find that most of them, without talking to each other, will give their people four meetings after which, if they have not seen significant change, they will turn them over to another counselor or tell them to come back when they're more ready.

Personally, I've given much more time than this but I'm not a senior pastor and I get their point. I think you need to tailor it to each person and their life situations. I resist formulas and rules. People are not cars. They are complex human beings with complex problems. I prefer to give them time enough to prove to me that their heart is or is not really in this. The hard part is actually doing it, cutting them loose.

You'll do yourself a big favor if you give them some lead time. In fact, tell them up front that counseling should not last longer than eight to ten weeks. That lets them know they need to get to work. If you are not seeing change after four weeks, ask them why this is so. Ask them if there's anything you could be doing differently. Ask them if there's anything they haven't told you that you should know. I've met with the couple separately at times because sometimes one will tell you something if the other is not present. That's wisdom and experience talking here. Separate them and meet with them, then come back together.

To sum that one up, if you're not seeing much change and it's been a significant amount of time, and you have nothing left to teach them, with a lot of love and grace, cut 'em loose. They need to know that they got fired as counselees. You're not going to go all Trump on them and say, *"You're fired."* This isn't TV. This is real life, but don't let them walk around thinking they're in counseling and working on things when they're not really working on anything. If you give them a lot of information but it isn't leading to transformation, something isn't right and they're not ready. So, do them a favor and cut 'em loose, in love.

The second, and very common situation is when they don't do their homework. If they don't do their homework several weeks in a row, you need to cut 'em loose. My senior pastor taught me early on that *if you're working harder than they are, this ain't going to work.* So, what do you do if they're not doing their homework?

The first week they come back, I take responsibility and assume they did not understand what was expected because I did not explain it well enough. The second week they come back without it done, I tell them that I will contact them in between our next sessions and ask them if it's done. If it's not done, we do not meet until they can call me and tell me it's done. Folks, people I'm describing now don't usually call me back.

The last possibility that's important to consider is when they don't do what you say. This is when you have given specific instructions and they just refuse to do it or they argue with you when they hear what you're telling

Lessons Learned

them to do. Stubborn spirits are proud and arrogant spirits. The best counselees are the ones who are humble and teachable. The stubborn and proud are headed for a fall (Prov. 16:18; 1 Cor. 10:12-14). If you sense this in your counselee, ask them about it. Tell them what you're seeing. Give them a chance to evaluate it for themselves. They will most likely end counseling on their own or they will come back with a new spirit about them. I've seen both. However you end it, end it with love and in a loving way.

Steve Mawhorter

Lessons Learned

Chapter 33

Much ado about nothing

(Prov. 26:1, 3, 4, 7, 8, 10, 11, 12)

We first started our ministry in 1998. At that time, there was only me and 5 female counselors. We were all green at the time, but God was gracious to us. Early on, He gave us cases that we could all handle. He didn't give us the clinically depressed, schizophrenics, adulterers, and so on. He gave us the run of the mill marriages struggling with communication or the depressed woman or the young guy stuck in pornography. Yes, these are hard things to deal with for people but they're not super complicated for counselors.

As time wore on, God has chosen to give us more and more hard situations like those above and while those are hard for sure, they are not what I would call the hardest. The hardest and most taxing ones are often the ones that last a long time but without much change.

These often involve people that you'd like if you met them on Sunday morning. In fact, they are the people that most people like. They are people who are often very involved and very visible in the church. But, while they are liked by most other people and also like most other people they know, they do not like each other. As I looked over my notes while preparing this chapter, I noticed a half dozen of these couples and it dawned on me, the longer our counseling relationship lasted, the less likely it was that it would improve. Let me illustrate.

Meet Casey and Kristen

Casey and Kristen both grew up in Christian homes but neither home was super Christian. By that, I mean, church attendance was evident but a love for the church was not. They believed in the Bible but did not read the Bible beyond Sunday morning. One grew up in a very controlling environment.

The other grew up in a free-for-all environment. The opposites from there just continued.

In preparing for marriage, they had determined they would not be like their parents. Guess what? They ended up just like their parents, warring about just about everything you can imagine, from the way the carpet is vacuumed to the way the fridge is organized. They fought about school choice, about women working outside the home, about the cost of air conditioning to the type of clothing they wore. The list is endless. I could go on and on and on.

I could give you many other couples like this but it's all the same. They make mountains out of molehills. Everything is a big deal. To quote Shakespeare for a moment, "they make much ado about nothing," and I mean nothing.

"You said you'd be home at 5:30 and it's 5:35!" "I never said 5:30. You thought I said 5:30."

"You said you'd clean the garage today." "No, I didn't." "Yes, you did!" "No, I didn't!" "Yes, you did!!"

I know you think I'm exaggerating. Trust me. I am not. Here's one you'll love.

The wife likes the room cold. The husband loves it warm. What's your counsel to them, counselor? Well, here's what they did. She would leave the window open when they went to sleep, and he would wait till she was asleep and then close the window. She would wake up in a stone cold sweat and open the window. He would wait till she's asleep again and open it. And so on, and so on. Same guy, just to spite his wife, would cut his fingernails and leave them on the counter just to make her mad. This is not made up stuff folks. They really did things like this!

Okay, here's another one you'll love (or hate). The wife struggles with keeping things orderly and clean. No problem, except that she's married to a guy with OCD. Their house is small, so they have to share an office. Can you see where this is going? C'mon God, say it ain't so. You paired a slob with an OCD guy and then made them share an office? Well, the husband was so frustrated with her sloppiness spilling over to what he saw as his side of the room, that he duct-taped it. She could do whatever she wanted with her side, but she could not step one foot on his side at all. I can hear some of you neat freaks out there saying, "What? What's wrong with that?"

Still, another guy who owned his own business used to pay all his bills late on purpose. He knew exactly which counterparty would fine him and when they would fine him so he would wait right up to the last day and then pay the bill. Now, some of you probably do that but you do that because you are robbing Peter to pay Paul. You're barely able to keep your finances together so this is what you have to do. Well, don't give my guy a break on this one. She hated the way he did that and would be the one to get the calls from the creditors. He knew she hated it and did it just to spite her. Yep, no kidding.

Folks, the list of this kind of childishness goes on and on. You might be wondering why they do this. To name a few reasons, some do it out of hatred. Some because they can't think of anything more devilish. To some, it's a form of entertainment. I guess there are a host of other reasons but whatever they are, it's ridiculous and makes my job impossible. There's a reason we don't counsel eight-year old kids. You can't reason with them because their brains are not fully formed. I contend there are some eight-year old brains in fifty-year old bodies. They are impossible. And, I mean that literally. So, what do you do with them?

I have a lot of success stories in this book and that's accurate. In fact, we figure that if you are part of our church, and you come for counseling, about eighty percent of you will do well. If you are from another church, we estimate that about fifty percent of you will do well. Of those twenty percent from our church or those fifty percent not from our church that do not do well, there is a very small percentage of those that are like these "eight-year old, fifty-year olds", but those few can make my life as a pastor very discouraging.

If I could do my counseling over again with these couples, I would have ended counseling much sooner. I've kept them as long as thirty weeks. Way, way, too long! I'm a patient person and I love people and I really believe God can change people and He wants to and will change all believers (Rom. 8:28-29; Col. 1:21; Heb. 13:21). And, I want to be used for that purpose. So, when I hear them bicker back and forth and back and forth, my patience, love, and faith overcomes my wisdom and I hang on too long, wasting everyone's time. So, you're wondering, "how do I know if I have one of *those* couples?"

The principle

If you're in weeks four to eight, it's not time to cut bait yet, but you're getting close. If you're in week twelve, and they're both digging their heals in, it's time to tell them that if they don't change real soon, you're done. If you're at week 16 or so, end it.

How this can help your ministry

Now these numbers are not exact, but you get the point. Don't be distracted by their nice demeanor towards you or the fact that others like them. That's what would happen to me. Believe what you see in front of you. Are they still bickering after twelve weeks of counseling, numerous hours of homework and a ton of prayer? If so, do the people on your wait list a favor and drop this couple. I know that sounds harsh to some of you, but is it? I'll let you decide on your own.

Cutting people like this loose (as we discussed in the previous chapter) will help you keep your own personal sanity. It will let the couple know they were bad counselees and it will communicate to other people in your church that we mean business when we counsel. God's commands are not to be taken lightly. If you give them specific assignments and they just blow right past them for weeks upon end, their hearts are not in it and they are just using you to get at the other or using you so they can save face in front of their friends because they are "getting counseling for their problems."

I've had a half dozen couples like this in my twenty plus years of counseling and not one of them has turned out for the better. Not one.

Lessons Learned

Chapter 34

Church discipline, does that really work?

(Matt. 18:15-17; Lk. 15:20; 2 Cor. 2:7)

We live in a day and age where everyone is so afraid to hurt someone's self-esteem that we have become afraid to follow simple guidelines that Jesus gave us and Paul showed us. Very few churches, even good churches, trust the Scriptures enough to apply church discipline to its members. This is not a new problem. It's what Paul ran into in Corinth with the young boy having sexual relations with his mother-in-law. When Paul got there, he found the church doing nothing about it, so he gave instructions drawn from principles taught by Jesus in Mathew Chapter 18:15-17.

Arguments against using church discipline are numerous. That was for then, not now. That was for Jews. We are Christians. It's too harsh. It won't work. People will leave my church if we do that. We'll get sued. Blah, b-blah, b-blah. I've heard it all. Don't listen to it.

Will people leave your church? Yes, but others will come. Several years ago, on a Sunday when we happened to be putting someone out of the church, two men who had been leaders at their previous church happened to be there at the service. They came up after the service. They were wearing suits, so I thought they were attorneys and were going to serve us papers. Nope. They were ecstatic that someone would finally trust God with His ways of doing things. They decided that day that our church would be their new home. They brought family members with them who brought other friends with them. We lost a couple of people that Sunday who disagreed with our decision, but we gained so much more.

Is it too harsh? Anyone who says that has never been a pastor or an elder. It is an emotionally excruciating process, that gobbles up an incredible amount of time for a ton of people. To do nothing would be harsh to the people who are being wounded by the person who is sinning. You have to pick who you're going to love. If you think you're loving the offender by not taking them before the church, then you are not loving the victim. We choose to believe that we are loving both by following the clear commands in Scripture.

Some question whether it will work. Yeah, we've heard that one, too. But, what is meant by the word, "work?" First, we don't do it because it will work. We do it because He told us to. Second, the work we do during the process of church discipline is our way of obeying the commands given. The real work is done by the Lord after we do ours. Why would we get in the way of what He's doing by not doing our part? Besides, it does work. We've had 3 people taken before the church who later repented. Here's one story.

Meet Fred and Ethel

Fred and Ethel had been married for many years and had 2 children. Both Mom and Dad were professing believers. The children attended church but had not professed faith as of yet. Mom started coming to our biblical counseling class called Cornerstone. She was growing fast and furious and while that is exciting to see, it often happens that God is preparing you for a difficult time ahead. And, boy, was that true.

A few years ago, Fred had been unfaithful. Ethel forgave him. Well, during Cornerstone, Ethel had some questions about forgiveness because she wasn't sure if she had really forgiven Fred. We had many talks after class about what that looks like. Shortly after that class ended, Fred was caught in another affair, this one more serious than the others.

As you can imagine, Ethel went berserk but she wasn't ready to leave the marriage. And somehow, Ethel had convinced Fred to meet with our senior pastor. Their meeting did not last long as Fred didn't have much to say and our senior pastor didn't have much hope for them. He sent them down to my office. I'm not sure what he thought I could accomplish that he couldn't.

When they got to my office, I found the same thing he did. Ethel was willing to forgive again but for Fred, that was a different story. There was absolutely no affect about him. He was emotionless. I saw nothing but darkness, such a darkness that I had never seen. He was gone. I'm not even sure why he was there. They left with little hope because that's all there was. A sad day for sure. I thought I'd never see him again.

Lessons Learned

Two weeks later, while sitting in church, I looked down my row and guess who I saw. Yep, it was Fred and guess who he was sitting with. Nope, not his wife. He was sitting with his girlfriend. Crazy, right?

Well, I knew what I needed to do and that was to tell Fred that he would need to find another church. We didn't take him all the way through formal discipline because he was not a member at the time, but we effactually did the same thing by removing him from the benefits and fellowship of the church.

On one hand, this was a hard call for me to make. No one likes putting someone out of the church. On the other hand, this was an easy call to make. We needed to take care of Ethel, who was a member, and her 2 children. This was their church and no longer his. So, I called him to tell him to find another church. His response was a classic.

He asked me, "when did the church start kicking out its members?" My response was two-fold. First, "you are not a member." Second, "the church should always have been removing members who are unrepentant adulterers." I think that caught him off guard a little but as I look back, I think he had enough truth in him to know it was the right thing for the church to do. His next response to that was also classic and very revealing at the same time.

Fred asked me for a recommendation on a good bible teaching church that he can go to. I know, a bunch of you are thinking, WHAT?! Is he out of his mind? He wasn't out of his mind. He was just blinded by sin like anyone of us can be. Grace and mercy, readers. Grace and mercy. I gave him 5 local churches that are teaching the Bible like we do. He picked one just a couple of miles away.

Several weeks later, I got a call from my pastor friend at that church. We had an interesting conversation regarding Fred. That pastor thought he saw a changed person. He was right. I met Fred for breakfast a month or so later. I didn't even recognize him. After being with him for an hour, I realized I had witnessed an amazing transformation.

You remember that my first meeting with him was a disaster. There was no affect in his face and no words from his mouth. He had nothing to say, literally nothing. Now, here I am at breakfast and I can't get him to shut up. We ate for 2 hours and I spoke for maybe 10 minutes. The rest was him, all him. God had totally changed him. He credits church discipline, which woke him up.

After my phone call with him, he went to the beach and broke down in tears. He realized, though he thought of himself as a Christian, he could not possibly be. God broke him that day at the beach and dropped the scales from his eyes. Fred was now a believer. Amen! We did our part and God did his. This man's soul was saved. So, what's become of Fred now?

Fred was welcomed back to the church. Ethel became a counselor. You can image how effective she can be when talking about forgiveness. Fred is now one of our adult Sunday school teachers and he is very well received. He gave his testimony before the church on an Easter Sunday and both children made professions of faith. Wow, right?

This happened because we trusted God with His commands. Do what's right, people. Love them enough to bring God's hand of discipline. You may save his life.

How this can help your ministry

The principle here is simple. Trust the Scriptures. Do what it says. When it comes to public, egregious, and unrepentant sin, go through the process God has given us as it is outlined in Matthew 18:15-17. We cannot call our people to repent of their sin if we, as a church, are not willing to repent of our own. This is not complicated folks. We just don't like the process and have let the world affect how we handle sin in our churches. Stop it. With love and in the most loving way possible, follow the guidelines He has given us. And, when they return as Fred did, welcome them with wide-open arms (Lk. 15:20; 2 Cor. 2:7). You won't be sorry.

Lessons Learned

Chapter 35

Should I work with a doctor or a psychiatrist?

Meet Tom and Kim

Tom and Kim are young but have been married for nearly ten years and have several kids. Kids and work keep them busy, but their marriage is solid. They love camping and had a great trip planned to Santa Cruz. When they got there, Kim started feeling sick, saying it almost felt like she was having a heart attack. She's only thirty-seven. How can this be, right?

Well, it got bad enough that they had to abandon the vacation and come home. They immediately went to the emergency room as the pain continued to worsen. Any time you even come close to mentioning chest pain, you're going to be admitted immediately, and she was.

After running a few tests, it turned out she only had gall stones but that they to be removed right away. So, no biggee, right? It's just a little gall bladder surgery. These happen all the time.

The surgery came and went successfully and they sent her home with a two-day supply of Norco, which contains a combination of acetaminophen and hydrocodone. Hydrocodone is an opioid pain medication. This should have helped her with any pain she might experience. Should be no problem and end of story. Not this time.

Kim had a bad reaction to the medication and probably to the anesthesia she was given for the surgery. She couldn't sleep for a week, sleeping only two hours at a time. She couldn't focus and would get agitated easily. About five days in, she started twitching and having irrational thoughts. Fun times for Tom, eh?

She was then given an anti-anxiety medication and that, too, backfired. Then, after a short meeting on the phone with a psychiatrist, she was given 20mg of prozak, an anti-depressant. Kim was getting more and more confused with each day. Remember, she's a solid girl and never had any problems like this before. Tom and Kim were very concerned. It was then that they called me.

Kim and I spoke over the phone and once in person. After our meeting, I set her up with a woman from our church who has over thirty-five years of experience in the psychiatric world. So that she doesn't get a hundred calls, I'll call her Sherrie. Every church needs a *Sherrie*.

Sherrie spent a little time with Kim and got her set up with another psychiatrist who ended up meeting with Kim for the next eighteen months. I also set Kim up with one of our counselors on staff. They met for six months. With help from her doctors, her husband, her counselor, and her psychiatrist, Kim would tell you now that it actually took about 18-24 months for her to totally recover from this mess.

This whole experience has proved extremely helpful to Kim. She would say that she has learned to know and trust God like she had never before. On top of that, it even improved her marriage. She didn't have a bad marriage. In fact, it was a good one. But, when this happened, she started having these crazy, irrational, yet believable to her, fears that her husband would leave her. What kind of man would stay with a woman with her kind of problems, right? After watching how he responded to her and cared for her, she felt more loved than ever before.

When I recently spoke to Kim about all this, I remarked that it would be fun to see if God has plans for her to use her experience for the good of someone else and wouldn't you know it, He already has. About six months into the experience, a friend from another church contacted her regarding a friend who was going through something similar. Kim contacted her and helped her through it. They are now lifelong friends. AND, that girl is now helping someone out with the same problem in the city where she now lives, a city that is one hundred miles away. God is good.

Wasn't this just a little gall bladder surgery?

The principles

I learned at least 3 things from this situation.

First, no surgery is just a simple surgery. Anytime, someone goes under the knife, so to speak, and is given medication of any kind, things can happen. You'll notice next time you go to the hospital and the Anesthesiology meets with you, that he has papers for you to sign. Those are essentially to inform you but mainly to cover their behinds. And, I'm sure you have had many friends go home with painkillers and everything is fine. Well, that's not true for everyone and it wasn't true for Kim. By the way, a side note, giving opioid painkillers to young people is a bad idea. Our country is just now learning this, but that's another chapter to write.

Second, I also learned that it does take a village, or the body of Christ, to help someone through a time like this. It doesn't matter how solid a person is spiritually. Kim was solid. But, Kim has a body just like you and me but her body reacted differently than mine would have. She needed advice from me, Sherrie, her counselor from church, her husband and yes, her psychiatrist, which brings me to the third thing I learned.

Third, in our biblical counseling world, there is an underlying mistrust of doctors, psychologists, and psychiatrists, and for good reasons. However, there are times when it can be helpful. In this case, as you have read, Kim's issue involved the body, soul, and the brain. Her bodily reaction to the medication and anesthesia played a factor. The way her brain is wired for stress and panic played a factor. And, the way she processed this information spiritually played a factor.

Together, with the help of the medical doctors, Sherrie, and our counseling ministry, this turned out very well for Kim. It's a great model for how we can work with the medical and psychiatric community around us. Don't be afraid to work with doctors and psychiatrists but don't leave your people to them without your involvement. Kim had Sherrie, me as her pastor, and Marcy, her counselor. That said, what do you do if you don't have a Sherrie?

How this can help your ministry

Get yourself a *Sherrie*! Don't sit around and complain about not having one. Don't give up on the idea. Get out there and find one. Make some calls to churches in your area. Google Christian psychiatrists. Meet them. Take them out to lunch. Hear what they think and believe about God, medicine, etc. Don't assume they are all the boogie man. In fact, assume they love God and want to help people. Then, invite them to your church. Invite them to a biblical counseling conference with you. Invest your time in them. You might be very surprised to find out you have a Sherrie in your community that you didn't know about.

This does not mean you cavalierly just throw your counselees to the doctors and hope for the best. In fact, if she's single or if she's a married woman whose husband can't be there, I would highly recommend that you go with your counselee to her doctor appointment so that facts can be affirmed and talked through.

We know that medications and psychiatrists who diagnose and prescribe are not the panacea to all of life's problems. In fact, they may even exacerbate the problems. However, there are those times, where they have proven to be helpful. To be clear, I do not think it wise for any person to be taking psychiatric medication without anyone knowing about it. Someone should be in the loop on this. Just don't throw out the baby with the bathwater every time.

Hopefully, this story will help you take surgeries seriously enough that you will enlist the help of many people and follow up on your people when it comes to medications.

Steve Mawhorter is available for interviews and personal appearances. For more information contact:

Steve Mawhorter
C/O Advantage Books
P.O. Box 160847
Altamonte Springs, FL 32716
info@advbooks.com

To purchase additional copies of this book visit our bookstore website at:
www.advbookstore.com

Longwood, Florida, USA
"we bring dreams to life"™
www.advbookstore.com

www.ingramcontent.com/pod-product-compliance
Lightning Source LLC
Chambersburg PA
CBHW060531100426
42743CB00009B/1497